Thank you
Matthew
for your Help

Ever

Bernmitta du Blan

RELIEF IN
RECOVERY

Stopping Depression, Anger and Relapse...Fast

Bernardo du Blanc

with Susan Claire

Cartoons and Illustrations by
Arnold D. Clapman

Foreword by Robert Newport, M.D.

Visual Books, Capitola, California

VISUAL BOOKS, 1840 41st Avenue, #102-133, Capitola, CA 95010 U.S.A. 408-475-2131
MANUFACTURED IN THE UNITED STATES OF AMERICA
Cartoons and Illustrations by Arnold D. Clapman

Library of Congress Cataloging-in-Publication Data
du Blanc, Bernardo, 1922-
Relief in Recovery: A proven system to stop depres-sion, anger & relapse among alcoholics and addicts/ Bernardo du Blanc - 1st ed.

240p. 23cm.
Bibliography: p. 216 - 218
Includes index
1. Alcoholism - Popular Works.
2. Drug Abuse - Psychological Aspects.
3. Depression, Mental - Treatment.
I. Title.

ISBN 1-887195-15-7 (PB): $17.95

10 9 8 7 6 5 4 3 2 1

First Edition

Dedication

Dedicated to the memory of my personal friend, the late Bill W., Co-Founder of Alcoholics Anonymous, whose encouragement and assistance many years ago enabled me to make the connection between diet, exercise, attitude, and my behavior. It has changed my life...

for that I am eternally grateful.

— Bernardo du Blanc

What's Between the Covers

Acknowledgments

I'd like to thank the following people for believing in me and helping me to publish this book:

Randy Baker M.D.
Michael Beresford
Michael M. Bauer
Sharon Clapman
Mel Chernev
Guthrie McRae Dodd
Mel Flyer
Barbara Gaughen
Gail Gay
Lorenzo Gold
Ben Handleman
Michael Harrison Esq.
John Kemp
Sandra Jo Kemp
Michael Kerrick
Hal Kramer
Paul Lind
Jerad MacLean
Linda Marcetti
Robert Newport, M.D.
Janice Keller Phelps M.D.
Daniel Phillips C.A.D.C.
Dan Poynter
Ramapriya Ruiz
Shana Ross
Simon Stapleton

Jay Sweet
Suzan Sweet
Robb Sals
Liz Scherle
Chuck Tedesco
Devi Treewater
Alice Williams
Kirby Wilkins Ph.D.
Burton Worrell O.D.

...and the thousands of people who have tried these techniques and told me about their relief.

Foreword

Hi there! You have in your hands a remarkable little book. It's short and sweet and if you've picked this book up because you need it, that is, you're in some sort of physical or emotional pain and you want to get better, this can help.

In simple-to-understand pictures and clear instructions, here is relief for most of what ails you. Bernardo's information is medically sound, based on years of research and experience of many scientists and doctors, of which I am one. It also reflects Bernardo's own experience. Bernardo has practiced what he has preached and is living a dynamic, energetic, fun-filled and passionate life! He is living proof of the success of his program. Bernardo would tell you, if you asked, that it took him ten years to get it all together, piecing together the information from a variety of doctors and trying out their advice. In the early days, advice on health, diets, smoking and exercise wasn't easy to get, but it is now.

Our nation's health as a whole is declining and people in all walks of life are concerned. Nutrition, life style, cardiac risk factors as well as depression and alcoholism/addiction are talked about openly, both in the media as well as in doctor's offices, but many, in fact, most people are in poor health. Many who are in pain or are still addicted or depressed won't go to a doctor's office (there wouldn't be nearly enough doctors if everyone did!) You are holding a book that can change your life if you follow its simple instructions.

Remember, what Bernardo has given you here is medically and spiritually sound AND it is proven. You WILL get relief when you make the choice to become responsible for your own body, changing your lifestyle and the habits that make you sick, and therefore make you miserable. If you're tired of being sick and miserable, and ready to get on with the business of living a healthy life, turn the page.

My best wishes for your good health,

Robert R. Newport, M.D.

About the Authors

Bernardo du Blanc has done research in the field of Biopsychology for over 30 years, with Drs. Abraham Hoffer, Hans Selye and Linus Pauling, among many others. He was a founding member of the California Orthomolecular Society. As a counselor in the field of drug and alcohol addiction for more than 40 years, he has worked with hundreds of people (and their doctors) to address the underlying physical causes of dysfunctional behavior and emotions. Their cases form the heart of this book. His experience as a humorous circuit speaker, and 42 years of sobriety fills the book with laughter and insight.

Susan Claire, founder of Visual books, assists authors in the self-publishing process. She was instrumental in the conceptual design of this graphic non-fiction format, in the editing of the manuscript and in the production of Relief in Recovery. As professional speaker and singer, Claire shares stories from personal experience as a Hypoglycemic. An MBA with 25 years experience in consulting and training, Claire has written 10 books, including Transforming Stress, Communication Dynamics and SuperVision.

Arnold D. Clapman is a gifted graphic artist who has produced fine art, illustrations for books, records and magazines, his own cartoon column, and animation for video games and national T.V. Networks. He is currently involved in developing a system which will refurbish and save classic films, has written original screen plays, and has published a training tape for conga drumming techniques.

Robert R. Newport, M.D. has an active psychiatry practice in Santa Cruz, California. His patients report successful use of his prescribed doses of Orthomolecular vitamins and amino acids to assist in healing the physical causes of dysfunctional emotional states.

Laine L. Berning, Chief Operating Officer of Visual Books, has served as project coordinator, editor, and creative consultant for this book.

IMPORTANT NOTICE

This book is not designed to give you all the information available on health issues. Rather it is meant to highlight common themes in research by experts in the health and recovery fields. If you are interested in more information, please see the references listed in the Appendix.

Some contents of this book are my personal opinion. I am not a medical doctor. On occasion, my opinion may differ from those of some medical professionals, they are based on my own research and experience.

This book is not intended as medical advice, or as a substitute for consultation with a licensed medical practitioner. Please don't try to diagnose yourself—leave that to the professionals. Everyone is biochemically different, not only in their heritage, but from day to day as their systems evolve. If you have any questions, ask your doctor.

There are a few cautions in this book; please read them carefully. When your friends see how good you look, and ask how you did it, give them your whole story—and a copy of this book.

—Bernardo du Blanc

The If Only Club

You have probably spent time in the secret club called "if only"... That's the club where your secret committee holds meetings in your head, usually in the middle of the night or real early in the morning.

Their voices are full of blame and shame, they point their fingers and say things like:

"If only you hadn't said those awful things."

"If only you weren't so shy."

"If only you hadn't gotten drunk."

"If only you weren't always so tired."

"If only you had more confidence."

"If only you didn't get violent."

"If only you weren't depressed all the time."

"If only you were like _____."

(you fill in the blank)

There's nothing like a meeting of the club to make you reach for a little drink, a lot of TV, or the Häagen-Dazs cure for depression.

To get the committee off your back, you may have already tried:

changing partners

changing jobs

changing towns

changing cars

changing doctors

inspirational books

12 step programs

losing weight

more sex

less sex

religion

counseling

Prozac

exercise

seminars

shopping

If any of these 16 options are bringing you even a little relief, for goodness sake don't stop what's working. The suggestions offered in this book are all completely natural. They are intended to enhance any spiritual, psychological or physical program you are following. I encourage you to advise your physician or counselor of any part of this book you are adding to your life.

The exciting thing is that by the time you have finished the first few chapters of this book, you can have a 72 hour Relief plan from the club.

Besides, this book has big type and lots of pictures so you can get to the "good part" in a hurry. You'll probably find yourself using this book regularly on your happy journey to relief.

Chapter 1

What's in This Book for You

In this book you'll find techniques that reduce anger, fear, depression and violence caused by the physical side of addiction. You'll find the latest research by medical experts in this field, true stories of folks who have found relief in recovery and my personal story of what worked for me over the past forty years.

I hope my story of how it was, the things I did that worked, and how it is now, is helpful to you.

I was free at last. Oh, what a feelin'!

My first ten years of sobriety were the kind of life you dream about—when you wake up, you're glad it was just a dream! The folks around me never knew whether I was gonna hit 'em or hug 'em, and neither did I. It was like being sober and still livin' in an invisible glass jail cell.

In my own effort to get the monkey off my back, I worked my spiritual program with all my heart. At the same time, I studied and learned all I could to get the squeaks out of my head. I spent so much darned time on a psychiatrist's couch, I got bedsores.

After years of all these actions, I was plagued with nutty behavior which screwed up my relationships and made me feel like warmed-over gravy down inside.

My mood swung from anger to depression, with naggin' self-pity and fears that interfered with my life. It wasn't until I learned the physical connection to these behaviors that I finally got a grip.

My mood swung from anger, to depression... It wasn't until I learned the physical connection to these behaviors that I finally got a grip.

I learned about how my messed up pituitary, pineal, thyroid, thymus and adrenal glands changed my behavior, first-hand, from several well-known health professionals whose names are listed at the end of this book.

But nothin' changed 'cause I kept on expectin' some of these great doctors to come and fix me...ZAP—just like that! When I finally realized my body can and does mend itself if I give it the right stuff—everythin' changed—not overnight, but gradually.

Things really changed when I finally started taking the vitamins and aminos like those listed in this book. When I really stayed with regular exercise, and a whole new food program, plus my daily prayer and meditation I realized I had a strength I never had before.

The results were mind blowin'! Talk about energy—my anger, fear and depression sure slowed down, my violence just stopped. I was able to cut way down on the fat, sugar, coffee, colas, white flour and even smoking. I simply calmed down and no longer made a supreme court case out of a parking ticket...I was free at last. Oh, what a feelin'!

But it didn't last! I began to notice (and so did those around me) every time I ate sugar, drank coffee or smoked cigarettes (which are loaded with sugar), I would act the same as I did when I was drinking even though I was sober. I started keeping my own Relief Recorder to track what I ate and how often I went nuts afterwards.

"...every time I ate sugar, drank coffee or smoked cigarettes, I would act the same as I did when I was drinkin' even though I was sober."

Things really changed when I stayed with these I.D.E.A.S.

During the last 40 years, I've tried hundreds of things and kept doing what worked and scrapped what didn't. That's how I.D.E.A.S. was born. Here's what I.D.E.A.S. stands for:

 INITIATIVE

 DIET

 EXERCISE

 ATTITUDE

 SERVICE

Check 'em out, one at a time, and see how I.D.E.A.S. can work for you.

INITIATIVE

Initiative—*Webster's* calls it "a first move". Well, by golly, you've already made a "first move" to take charge of your emotions and addictions when you bought this book, and then read this far. Nice going. (Ps-s-s-t...you'll learn a lot more about Initiative in the Initiative chapter, but I'll tell you this; I.D.E.A.S. wouldn't be the same without Initiative, cause nothin' happens if nothin' happens.)

Ps-s-s-t...

DIET

Diet—is not a four-letter word for starvation. Webster calls diet "food, or to eat." That got your attention, didn't it? And the good news is the Diet chapter is not about goin' hungry or doin' without, it's about eatin' good and feelin' good!

In the Diet chapter, you'll get the lowdown on which foods and drinks can make your fangs come down, or make you want to snooze, and which make you want to crawl in a hole and pull the hole in after you.

Diet is not about giving up food. It's about substituting good stuff for the junk food that makes you nuts. Interested? You can even take the Initiative to skip the Initiative chapter and go right to the Diet chapter to learn about which foods make your life more fun.

In the Diet chapter you'll get the lowdown on which foods and drinks can make your fangs come down...

...and which make you want to crawl in a hole and pull the hole in after you.

EXERCISE

You and I are exercisin' to live free of anger, depression, anxiety and wild mood swings—right?

Exercise—Everythin' I had ever read about exercise praises those who do it and makes the other 90% feel guilty. So I have come up with exercises where "every body" wins.

Don't go skipping this chapter to "get to the good stuff"—because this chapter *is* the "good stuff". Here you learn how to go from where you are now and custom design your own exercise program. After all, my friend, we ain't exercisin' to get oohs or ahs or to lose weight...you and I are exercisin' to live free of anger, depression, anxiety and wild mood swings—right?

ATTITUDE

We've kicked ourselves so much over our behavior, it's a wonder both our legs aren't double-jointed.

Attitude—This chapter is to help you change your attitude about the one you see in the mirror. Most of us with deep emotional problems and physical addictions have kicked ourselves so much over our behavior, it's a wonder both our legs aren't double-jointed.

In the Attitude chapter you'll get some real tools to help you kick out those free-loaders hanging out in your head, making you wrong. You know who I mean: the twins Blame and Shame, Old Guilt and Cousin Worry. They're all kept in line by Nellie Need-for-Approval.

If you use the tricks you learned in Initiative, Diet, Exercise and Attitude; you're gonna be walkin' around with such a big grin that folks'll think you've got a feather in your drawers.

SERVICE

Service wasn't added to make the acronym I.D.E.A.S. come out right. It's in here 'cause I learned the hard way that doin' for, or thinkin' of somebody else kept my mind off my own problems. I also know it's hard to think of somebody else when you've got a 10,000-pound elephant standin' on your foot.

When "Jumbo" was weighin' me down with emotional pain and embarrassment over my behavior, I see-sawed between fear, hopelessness, self-pity and isolation.

It's hard to think of someone else when you've got a 10,000 pound elephant standin' on your foot.

I learned I couldn't wait around to get Jumbo off my foot before reaching out to others. Much to my surprise, when I reached out to share with someone else, Jumbo seemed to get lighter. I'll make you a promise. When you have made Initiative, Diet, Exercise and Attitude a part of your life, you will know in your heart why Service is such an important part of your Relief Program. I'll bet you'll want to share your own miracle too.

When I reached out to share with someone else, Jumbo seemed to get lighter.

Here are a couple more true stories from the thousands who have found relief through these I.D.E.A.S. One about depression and one about anger—emotions most of us in recovery can relate to.

Chapter 2

The Depressed Guy
a True
Story

C arl was given early retirement after 24 years on his job because doctors determined he was suffering from work-related stress. He's 53 years old, has a comfortable lifetime pension and now works part-time.

In spite of his 12 years in recovery, Carl has ongoing bouts with depression and wild mood swings. Carl has taken a variety of prescription drugs which only make him worse.

His wife invited me over because Carl seemed to be getting worse since taking Prozac.

As we look in, Brenda and I are in the dining room while Carl is sitting and staring out the window.

When I was a kid, I used a three-legged stool to milk our cow. One rainy day, one of the legs broke off and I tried to use the stool with two legs...

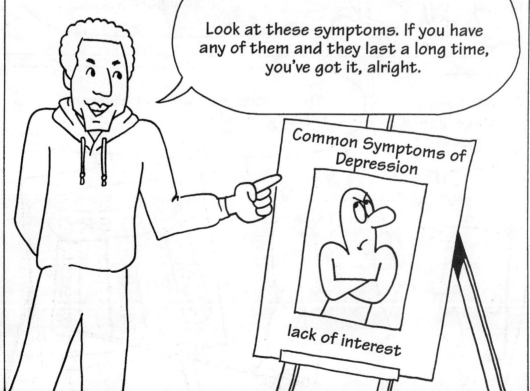

CHART # 1
COMMON SYMPTOMS OF DEPRESSION

anger

anxiety

fatigue

headaches

indecisiveness

Insomnia

irritable

sadness

poor
concentration

poor memory

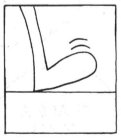

restless

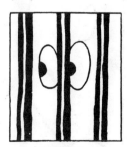

isolation,
withdrawal

COMMON SYMPTOMS OF DEPRESSION, CONT'D.

stomach troubles

suicidal thoughts

weight loss, gain

worrying

Boy, I never noticed the "big book" talks about the physical side. All right, you've got my interest.
WHAT DID BILL W. DO ABOUT HIS DEPRESSION?

In 1968 he told me after all his searching for a "mental cure", when he finally just cut back on coffee, cigarettes, and sugar, started eating better, taking vitamins, and walking a little...

...his depression let up.

I just can't imagine life without coffee, cigarettes and sugar. Are you sure that's my answer?

That'll cut down on your low blood sugar (Hypoglycemia), one of the main causes of depression.

Studies show most alkies are Hypoglycemic. Check out chart 2 which shows how Hypoglycemia can be hiding as depression.

SYMPTOMS OF HYPOGLYCEMIA AND DEPRESSION

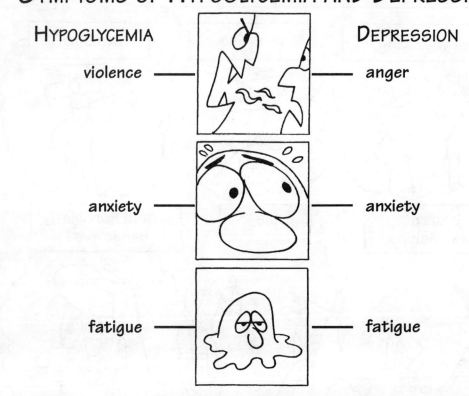

HYPOGLYCEMIA		DEPRESSION
violence		anger
anxiety		anxiety
fatigue		fatigue

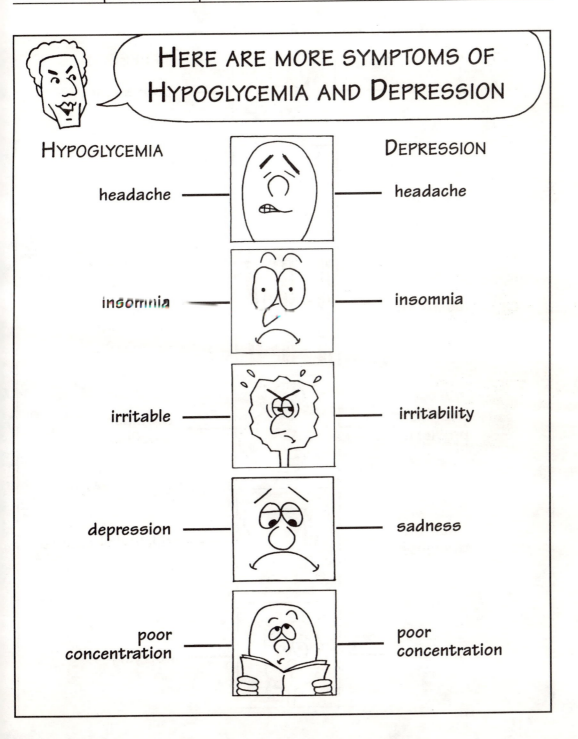

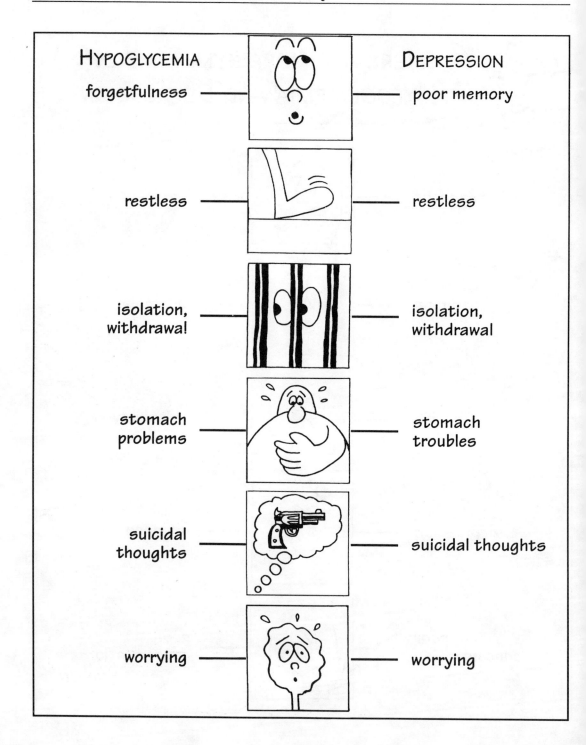

Chapter 3

The Angry Woman

Sandra is a 46-year old professional woman living in a nice home in an upper middle class neighborhood overlooking the Monterey Bay.

Sandra gave up alcohol and drugs (including nicotine) several years ago.

At the time of the incident which follows, Sandra was still drinking several cups of coffee daily and downing lots of sugar, white flour and fat. She was not exercising.

She had gained weight and had recently entered into a turbulent marriage.

And now join me and Sandra—the Angry Woman.

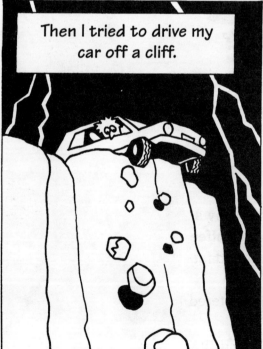

Today I woke up so depressed and hopeless, I decided to go to a mental hospital.

At the last minute, I decided to call you and see if you had any suggestions.

Sandra, would you do something that sounds a little strange in order to be calm in just 10 MINUTES?

WELL OF COURSE I WOULD!

Then put the phone down, go get a pinch of salt, place it on your tongue, let it dissolve and then we'll talk.

ALL RIGHT, NOW What?

That's all for now. Tell me, Sandra, did you try the Häagen Dazs cure for depression last night?

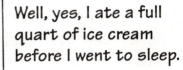

Well, yes, I ate a full quart of ice cream before I went to sleep.

How much coffee did you drink yesterday and today?

Oh, I had about 4 cups yesterday and 2 this morning.

How many cigarettes?

Oh, I quit smoking, but I chew about 3 packs of gum a day.

All that gum is loaded with about 30 % sugar. Your husband still smokes? Then you still smoke, too, and cigarettes are up to 75% sugar.

Sugar exhausts your adrenals.

When you pig out on ice cream, do you sometimes ask yourself, "Why am I doing this?"

Well, yes.

And when you scream terrible things at Darrel or your daughter, do you find yourself wondering why you are saying these things and secretly beating yourself up for it?

Yes.

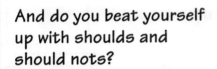

And do you beat yourself up with shoulds and should nots?

That's me all right.

Do you sometimes walk around filled with anger, not aimed at anything or anybody?

How'd you know?

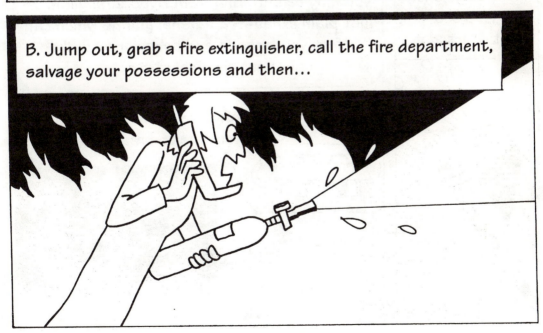

C. Ask the fire experts how it started and follow their advice about preventing another fire?

The salt was your fire extinguisher, now let's see what started it.

If you have one or more of these symptoms, you may be suffering from Hypoadrenalism or just plain exhausted adrenal glands which can affect your moods and behavior as well as your physical state.

Any one of these can cause your fire to break out again.

SYMPTOMS OF HYPOADRENALISM

fatigue

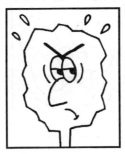

nervousness &
irritability

Premenstrual
Tension

craving for salt

mental
depression

craving for
sweets

allergies

headache

apprehensions

alcohol and drug
intolerance

weakness

pain in the neck
and trapezius
muscles

MORE SYMPTOMS OF HYPOADRENALISM

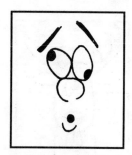

intervals of
confusion

poor memory

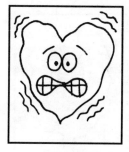

Heart Palpitation

stomach
problems

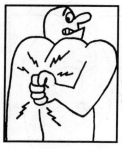

backache

light-headedness

constipation or
diarrhea

faintness or
fainting spells

Insomnia

Dermatitis

shyness

Hyperactivity

violence

Postural
Hypotension
(slump)

skin dry or thin

perspiration
scanty

overweight

sparse body hair

underweight

suicidal
tendencies

Great Caesar's Ghost, I've got half of those symptoms!

Hypoadrenalism is such a big word...what does it mean?

It just means that Adrea 'n' Al, your two tiny Adrenal glands, are lyin' down panting instead of doing their job.

What can I do to get them up off their butts? How about mind altering drugs...

...would that help?

Mind altering drugs are just what the name implies—they alter your mind to alter your reactions. Unfortunately...

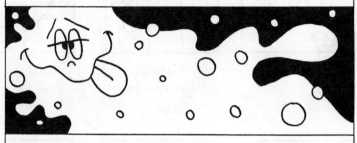

...if you like the effect, your doctor may renew them and you can become addicted. Then you still haven't corrected the problem —only the symptoms.

It's like putting a concrete shell over your burned out house— it looks good on the outside, but nothing has been done to locate the cause of the fire and rebuild.

And if you ever remove the concrete shell...

your smoldering home may burst into flames again.

Then I'd probably listen.

Its simple—
just do what it says in the Diet and Exercise chapters. It will work FAST!

This is what has worked for me for over 30 years.

I also told her to work with her physician to perform certain tests and monitor her progress.

Chapter 4

How Your Survival Team Works

T he purpose of this book is to help you see if something physical may be contributing to your erratic emotional behavior, and/or mental or physical pain so you can take steps to fix it—fast.

Your first step is to learn how that marvelous machine called your body/mind works. You won't have to go to medical school to learn about one part of your system which is key to mental/physical and emotional balance; all you have to do is turn the pages.

YOUR SURVIVAL TEAM AND HOW THEY WORK TO KEEP YOU HEALTHY AND HAPPY

Meet your Survival Team. This is an appropriate nick-name for the system of endocrine glands that works together to regulate the functioning of your body, emotions and your mind. "Endocrine" simply means they have no "duct" or exit. They each pump their chemicals directly into your blood stream. They each look different and they're located in different parts of your body. Once you have a general idea of how they work, you'll be able to see how you can help your Survival Team to improve your "disposition, efficiency, and even your personality"[1].

The Big Boss of your survival team is a "hard drivin" gland we'll call **Harry Hypothalamus.** He has a private office in your brain's center of tasting, hearing, and feeling. Hard-nosed Harry calls the shots that link your body and mind. And all this time you thought you called the shots!

The Big Boss of your survival team is a "hard drivin" gland we'll call Harry Hypothalamus.

Maestro Pineal—This midget conductor or third eye sits right on the front of your brain between your baby blues. The Maestro actually sneaks light right through your eye's retina so the Maestro can see the sheet music.

Maestro Pineal conducts.

The Maestro conducts all the other gland members to create the right mood music to help you sleep better and enjoy the trip more when you're awake.

Pat Pituitary works just down the hall from Harry and reports directly to him. Pat is no bigger than a green pea, but that little gal controls all the other survival team glands with over a dozen different chemicals called hormones

Pat Pituitary controls all the other glands...

Captain Timothy Thyroid shares an office with four to eight parathyroids down deep in your throat. He is round and red and about the size of a small oyster. His side-kicks are the parathyroids, which are the size of BBs from an air-rifle. We call him Captain because he controls your metabolism level and your energy. And get this: he has a lot to say about your moods and emotions. This heavy duty character puts out fires and tries to keep all systems going.

Captain Timothy Thyroid controls your metabolism.

Arnold Thymus lives downstairs under Capt'n Tim. This powerful body-builder uses your bone marrow to make *ten trillion chemicals* a day to keep your white blood cells healthy.

Your white blood cells are the good guys in the white hats who keep the bad guys out so you don't come down with something you can't even pronounce.

Arnold Thymus keeps your white blood cells healthy.

Dr. Peter Pancreas
controls the level of sugar
in your blood.

Adrea 'n' Al, the adrenals,
regulate your disposition.

When you experience
mental or physical stress,
Adrea 'n' Al increase your
blood pressure.

Dr. Peter Pancreas (located against the back wall of your abdomen) has tiny "islets" that pump out insulin to control the level of blood sugar in your bloodstream, so that your body has energy and your brain cells have fuel to work. Low blood sugar (Hypoglycemia) can mean that Doc Pancreas is sending too much insulin when you eat something sweet, and so you "can't think", because your brain is out of fuel. Once this "mad scientist's" regulator starts swinging too wildly, ol' Doc can stop sending any insulin, which means you have the condition called Diabetes.

Many blood sugar problems actually start with this next pair of characters. These two little super heroes, **Adrea 'n' Al**, are tiny pear-shaped adrenal glands that hang out on top of your kidneys[2]. These little rascals pump out 32 chemicals constantly that regulate your disposition, your efficiency and even your personality. They're little, but they sure do bully the other glands.

You can live (after a fashion) without any of the other glands, but not without Adrea 'n' Al. When they stop pumping, "it's all over but the soft music, slow walkin' and you in a pine box" as they say down South.

Adrea 'n' Al have to take all the food you eat and try to make it into usable building blocks (amino acids) that also affect the way you think and act.

When you experience mental or physical stress, Harry Hypothalamus sends a message to Adrea 'n' Al to pump out a chemical that will increase your heart beat and narrow your blood vessels so blood is going through them at a higher force (higher blood pressure). This adrenal chemical also relaxes and enlarges airways so your lungs can take in more air, more quickly.

When this adrenal chemical reaches Pat Pituitary, it causes your "master chemist" to pump out hormones that cause your adrenal casings, Captain Thyroid, the parathyroids, and even your sex glands to pump out their chemicals. All these chemicals prepare your body and mind to instantly deal with stress.

Sometimes the end results are seemingly superhuman feats of muscular strength and quick thinking.

Then there's the two we giggle or whisper about: **Ovaries and Testes**. You came equipped with one or the other (hopefully) of these sex glands. These glands do more than help you in the bedroom; they also make hormones that affect the way you look and also how you feel.

Ovaries and Testes make hormones that affect the way you look and also how you feel.

Now let's look at how this all fits together. Let me introduce you to:

Junk Food George.

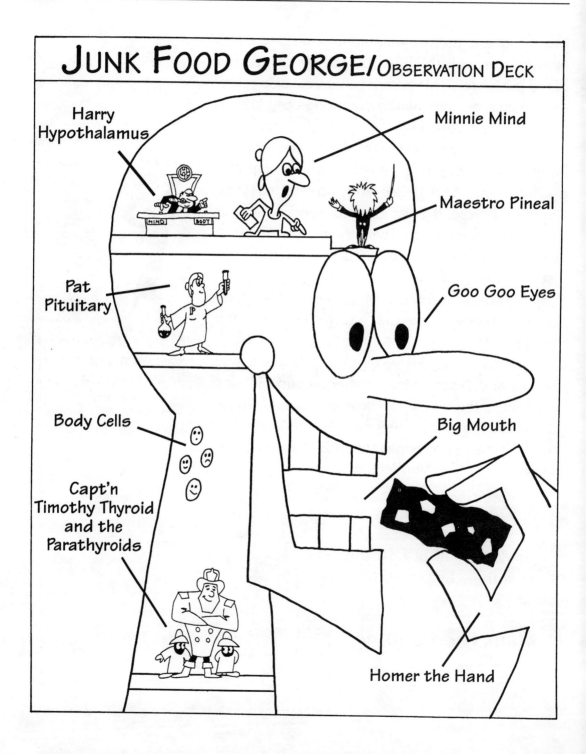

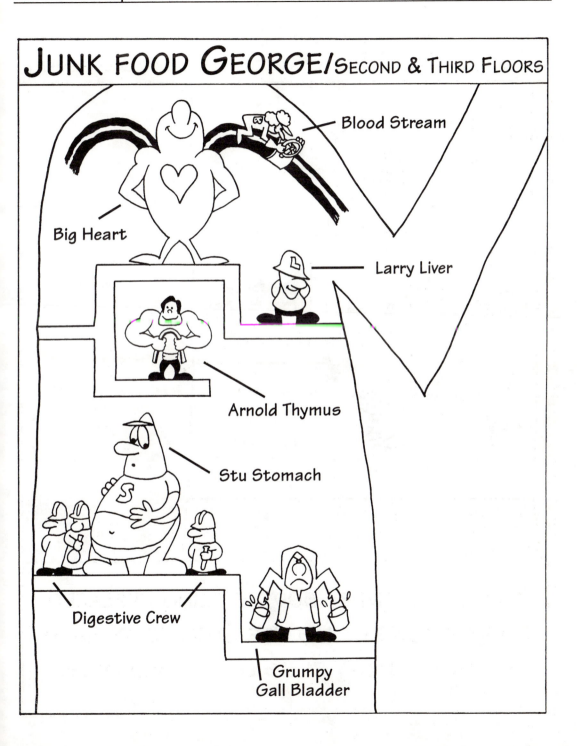

JUNK FOOD GEORGE/SECOND & THIRD FLOORS

Blood Stream

Big Heart

Larry Liver

Arnold Thymus

Stu Stomach

Digestive Crew

Grumpy
Gall Bladder

JUNK FOOD GEORGE/First Floor & Basement

THIS GUY'S ENTIRE BODY IS BEING REPLACED EVERY SECOND OF HIS LIFE. IT'S PRETTY HARD TO MAKE QUALITY PARTS OUT OF BROWNIES.

Chapter 5

Junk Food George

Your survival team works seven days a week, 24 hours a day, making chemicals and tossin' 'em back and forth with each other. We're talkin' about mass production. These hard working heroes turn out over 13 trillion chemicals every day. With all that volume and so many high performing players; split-second coordination is the norm. They make Japanese factories look like they're movin' in slow motion.

When one or more of your survival team players gets pooped, there ain't nobody waitin' in line to take their place. The rest of the gang tries to keep up without a full team and all hell breaks loose. Your pooped-out team then sends you a message. It's called physical and/or emotional pain.

To see what I mean, let's follow a brownie going down through Junk Food George.

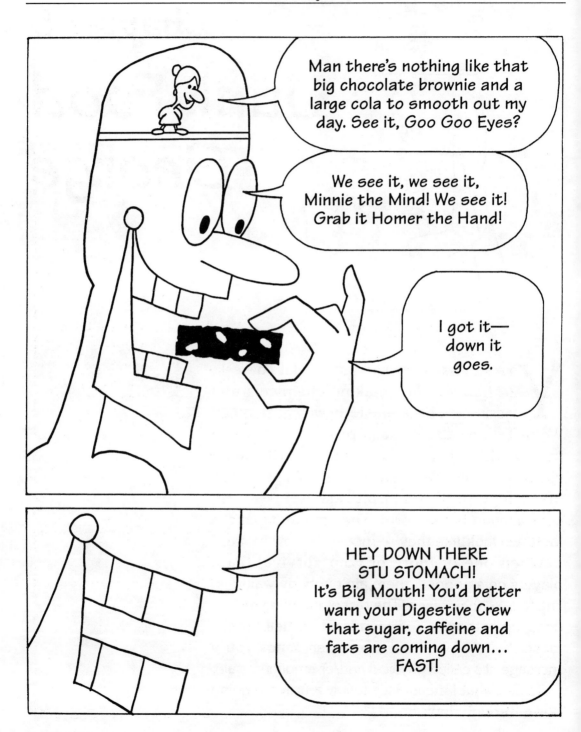

DIGESTIVE CREW

PAT PITUITARY

Don't tell Harry Hypothalamus what's going on down there or he'll throw one of his fits and let Minnie the Mind in on it...

THEN IT'S HELL TO PAY ON THE OUTSIDE.

We won't have to tell him. He'll know as soon as Stu Stomach gets this last load of sugar and poor ol' Doc Pancreas flips out trying to balance this guy's blood sugar and insulin.

BLOOD STREAM

Just look at poor ol' Doc Pancreas now. He's wobblin' back and forth like the town drunk, trying to do his ol' glucose/insulin balancing act.

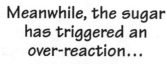

Meanwhile, the sugar has triggered an over-reaction...

and I've got too much insulin to get glucose out to the Body Cells.

Hey Blood Stream, we got millions of mouths to feed down here—where is our glucose fix? Without it, George is gonna be hunting for a hole to hide in.

Hey Doc, Body Cells are hollering for a glucose fix; I GOTTA HAVE LESS INSULIN RIGHT AWAY!

DOC PANCREAS

What a job—hurry up Doc, more insulin, less glucose; slow down Doc, less insulin, more glucose. Hmph, I should have taken early retirement the last time George overdid it!

HYPO GLYCEMIA

HARRY HYPOTHALAMUS

Hey Capt'n Thyroid, better turn up the heat and tell Doc Pancreas to get some more blood sugar to the brain right away...otherwise I'll have to make George angry to get some adrenalin going.

Doc says "YOU GOTTA BE KIDDING, Harry!" He's still staggering from the last load of sugar. Adrea 'n' Al, the Adrenals, are no help; they're just beat and laying down on the job. I'll ask Blood Stream for help.

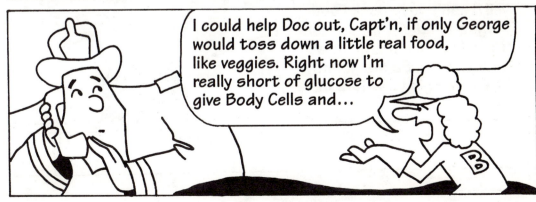

I could help Doc out, Capt'n, if only George would toss down a little real food, like veggies. Right now I'm really short of glucose to give Body Cells and...

Chapter 6
What Can Cause It

If anybody on your survival team gets sick or lazy, the whole bloomin' team has to work harder, and sometimes other team members can get sick too, trying to keep up. You know, the ol' domino effect. It's usually best to start out by lookin' at the super stars—Adrea 'n' Al and Tim.

First, let's look at what causes Adrea 'n' Al to get exhausted and lead you straight down into the "If Only" club.

According to Dr. John Tintera, a renowned endocrinologist, there are three ways Adrea 'n' Al can get worn out. The doctors call this Hypoadrenalism or Hypoadrenal Corticism.

You may have gotten Hypoadrenalism while your Mom was pregnant.

The first kind happens 'cause your Mom was Hypoadrenal while she was pregnant. Then you could have gotten a life threatening form of Hypoadrenalism or Hypoadrenal Corticism before you even got here. If that was true, you apparently lived through it, congratulations! But listen to this: you may arrive in this world without a trace of Hypoadrenalism and then it can show up in your adult life, WHAM, right when you least expect it. This form is called Congenital Hypoadrenalism. Ain't that a kick?

The second kind is called Constitutional Hypoadrenalism, which means you were born with a puny Adrea 'n' Al that could become pooped real easily. You're like a walking time bomb, you could suddenly develop Hypoadrenalism which could cause Hypoglycemia (low blood sugar) or adult onset diabetes (Hyperadrenalism). Oh, boy, lucky you!

The third kind is Lifestyle Related Hypoadrenalism, brought on by what you eat and drink, how you handle stress and how much exercise you don't get. Uh oh, gotcha.

No matter which one of these little jewels you may have, medical types say that Adrea 'n' Al, your two tiny adrenal glands, no bigger 'n' a pencil eraser, have a lot to do with your emotional highs and lows. How many of these 16 things are kickin' Adrea 'n' Al around in your bod?

If you have Constitutional Hypoadrenalism, you're like a walking time bomb.

Lifestyle Related Hypoadrenalism—16 Contributing Factors

pregnancy

childbirth

PMS

excess stress

illness; surgery

too little
exercise

air or water
pollution

lack of
sleep

alcohol

drugs

anger,
violence

junk food,
white flour

coffee

cigarettes

fat

sugar

If any one of your survival team is lyin' down on the job or you're into crazy eating, you can become Hypoglycemic. So...what is Hypoglycemia?

HYPOGLYCEMIA is a fancy word for low blood sugar. Just how important is Hypoglycemia? Well, the brain is fed only by glucose (blood sugar) and doesn't store any of that precious ol' glucose. This means the brain counts on a constant supply of blood sugar from the bloodstream. So having Hypoglycemia (low blood sugar) is a bummer for the brain.

"There is probably no illness today which causes such widespread suffering, so much inefficiency and loss of time, so many accidents, so many family break-ups, and so many suicides as that of Hypoglycemia."

—*Dr. Stephen P. Gyland, 1957*

Hypoglycemia is a condition, not a disease, so say the medical types. Whatever it is, more than 90% of the program people they tested have it, according to Dr. Joan Larson and Dr. Keith Sehnert. If you do, it can really rain on your parade.

If you have a hunch Hypoglycemia (or low blood sugar) may be your problem, check it out in the next few pages. Then talk to your doc about the need for testing and treatment.

Lookin' for a fast and safe way for quick relief from Hypoglycemia? Go ahead and talk with your doc, get busy with your Relief Recorder and the basic I.D.E.A.S. for Relief Program outlined in this book. Besides, if you're hurtin' the way I used to, getting over Hypoglycemia in a hurry could feel better'n winnin' the lottery.

> *"Hyperglycemia (high blood sugar) does not represent nearly as immediate a threat to the well-being of the body as does Hypoglycemia (low blood sugar)".*[1]
> —*S. Soskin, M.D.*

You saw some basic symptoms of Hypo-glycemia in the story of the Depressed Guy. Here are a few more.

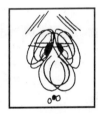

sweating   hunger   incoherent   blurred
                                   speech   vision

> *"Man may be the captain of his fate, but he is also the victim of his blood sugar."*
> —*Winfred G. Oakley, London 1962*

As if all the other symptoms of Hypoglycemia weren't enough, if your Hypoglycemia gets to be chronic a whole bunch of other symptoms may turn up, contributing to:

personality changes

maniacal behavior

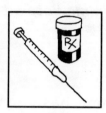

addiction/ Alcoholism

emotional instability

negativism

allergies

high IQ. kids labeled "under achievers"

nervous breakdown

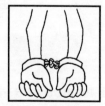

juvenile delinquency

PMS

backache

Schizophrenia

WHAT CAN CAUSE HYPOGLYCEMIA?

- Eating too much junk food (fed Hypo-glycemia).

- Adrea 'n' Al are pooped.

- Capt'n Tim is pooped.

- Screwed up enzymes that mess up your body's handling of fructose and all sugar.

- Diseases like hepatitis, cancer and cirrhosis of the liver.

- Too much exercise for too long.

- Pat Pituitary is goofing off or going out.

- Ol' Pete Pancreas is laying down loafing, or he is jumping around too fast.

- Something is shooting out your wiring (some type of nerve damage).

- Pregnancy, lactation, diarrhea or starvation (ain't that a mix).

Fed Hypoglycemia is caused by eating too much junk food.

"It is difficult to believe that such a little thing as eating too many sweets, something so many people do all the time, can have such dangerous potential consequences. And yet, this is not scare talk or exaggeration; it is scientific fact, documented by experimental evidence."

—*Josef P. Hrachovec, M.D.*

Anybody at any age can get Hypoglycemia and this even includes newborn babies.

CAN GRANDPA & BABY BOTH GET IT?

Anybody at any age can get Hypoglycemia and this even includes newborn babies. Better check that newborn babe if mom is Hypoglycemic. Moms who have the Rh Negative blood condition better talk it over with their docs so they can watch out for possible Hypoglycemia in the newborn babe. Infants who are either premature or full-term but low birth weight are also prone to Hypoglycemia. Undetected and untreated Hypoglycemia in babies can cause serious damage to the brain—so watch it!

Hypoglycemia turns up in a lot of my peer group (seniors) for a variety of reasons:

1. Hypoglycemic seniors don't exercise enough, so they develop dropsy and heart trouble—you know, drop the butt in a chair and haven't got the heart to pick it up!

2. A lot of the medications seniors take (and healthy seniors take an average of 3 to 5 a day) can drop their blood sugar.

3. The percentage of closet drinkers is very, very, very high among seniors.

4. Many seniors are not eating right and don't drink enough good water.

5. Our digestive system slows down with all those miles we put on it, so our food doesn't do us as much good for us as it did when we were younger.

6. Most of my peer group of seniors aren't taking enough vitamins to make up for this nutritional shortage. We older models need more vitamins.

7. Folks think of us seniors as always calm like a Norman Rockwell painting, but growin' old and losin' loved ones is hard work and we end up all stressed out.

Any one of these little jewels can set off Hypoglycemic depression except our doc usually treats the depression and doesn't ever look for the Hypoglycemia.

Next, let's look at Capt'n Tim. When Adrea 'n' Al (or any other Survival Team gland) lie down on the job it can sometimes cause Capt'n Tim to get overworked. Capt'n Tim can get overworked other ways too, and he is an important guy. His job includes getting oxygen to your brain and controlling your body temperature. He also plays a supporting role in keeping your weight down. So, keepin' him healthy is important.

All depression could be eliminated if the thyroid was working properly and getting adequate oxygen to the brain."

—Linus Pauling, M.D.

SYMPTOMS OF A POOPED CAPT'N TIM THYROID

mental
sluggishness

dry skin

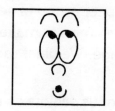

poor memory

fatigue

low sex drive

brittle hair

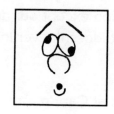

confusion

puffiness
around eyes

cold hands
and feet

sleeping more
than 8 hours

easy to catch
colds

weight gain

So much for symptoms—lets look at a few causes. Some of the craziest things can cause ol' Capt'n Tim Thyroid to get pooped. Look at this list:

X-rays

mammograms

dust and/or dirty air

too many prescription drugs

not enough Vitamin A, E, and Zinc

lazy Pat Pituitary

Because Capt'n Tim works your body's thermostat, one clue that he's not working well is that you get cold.

This chapter listed the main causes of you feelin' poorly. Remember, though, any member of your survival team can cause problems if they get lazy. Come with me and we'll look at ways to check it out.

Chapter 7

How to Check It Out ...Fast

We'll check out Adrea 'n' Al first, Hypoglycemia second and Capt'n Tim Thyroid third. You may then want to check out your whole survival team.

Let's start with Adrea 'n' Al. If you saw yourself in any those many faces in the previous chapters, check out your ol' bod for Hypoadrenalism (exhausted adrenal glands). Over 80–95% of alkies and 67% of other folks have it[1]. Exhausted adrenals can cause Hypoglycemia (low blood sugar), sugar and drug addiction, alcohol and food addiction, and all the sweat and pain that goes with 'em. Hypoadrenalism can drag down your whole glandular survival team's performance (especially Capt'n Thyroid) leavin' you with low thyroid, to boot.

Doctors have taught me a couple of simple methods for testing and treating exhausted adrenals and Hypoglycemia.

THE BEST TEST FOR LAZY ADREA 'N' AL & HYPOGLYCEMIA

YOU BE THE TEST TUBE

This test you paid for when you bought this book. You're the test tube when you read the book—especially the I.D.E.A.S. chapters and use what you learn. Most folks who follow the Relief program detailed in the I.D.E.A.S. chapters faithfully (the way you follow your favorite TV program), and keep a Relief Recorder (*Chapter 9*) or diary, notice people around them gettin' a darned sight nicer in just 3 to 5 days.

In as little as 72 hours most people who follow the Relief program usually feel better all over. They have more pep; their eyes begin to sparkle unless they've been sneaking sugar, fries, coffee or drugs. Now, you wouldn't do that, would ya?

Since the Relief program is a natural lifestyle, doctors agree most folks can safely go for the gusto and really follow the Relief program in this book for at least 30 days (I always remind 'em to first check in with their doc!).

That doesn't mean they stopped their program after 30 days! They kept goin'! It's the nature of this "hypo" ailment to play with their heads and tell 'em, "You're feeling better now, you can slack off." I've shared my Relief program with hundreds of

The Relief program is a natural lifestyle; doctors agree most folks can safely go for the gusto...

"hypos" over the last forty years, and some of 'em stopped doing the things that brought 'em relief as soon as they began feeling good. Sure 'nuff, the old 'moods' came back.

I've noticed that people who didn't keep track of what brought them relief were less likely to keep with the I.D.E.A.S.—that's why I created the Relief Recorder. This little book helps folks get the "connection" between their eating and exercising and how this *reeeally* affects their moods.

Most folks use their Relief Recorder for at least 30 days—'till they are used to all this new stuff. Some also need to check out their crazy thinking—so they tie up with a good shrink at the same time and tell him or her about the Relief program, their past history, their reactions and all that stuff.

When they stopped doin' the things that brought 'em relief...

...sure 'nuff, the old 'moods' came back.

A GOOD TEST FOR LAZY ADREA 'N' AL

Home Blood Pressure Test

Here's a simple test for Hypoadrenalism I do right in my own home. All I need for this is a blood pressure measurin' device for my arm, costin' about $18.00 at a drug store, and I have a do-it-yourself adrenal gland function test. I take two

I do a simple test for Hypoadrenalism right in my own home.

I take two blood pressure readings—one while I'm lying down and one while standing up.

blood pressure readings—one while I'm lying down and one while standing up.

Here's how I do it: rest for five minutes lyin' down before taking the reading. Then stand up and immediately take my blood pressure again. The normal systolic blood pressure (the higher pressure, for example 120/80) is about 10 mm higher when I'm standing than when I'm lying down. If my blood pressure is lower after standing, then Adrea 'n' Al are probably lyin' down on the job.

Women or teenage girls constantly having a systolic blood pressure reading (that's the first/higher number in a blood pressure reading) below 105 and men or teenage boys below 110 should see a doc for a complete Hypoadrenalism check up. Remember, any Hypoadrenalism test is not a test for Hypoglycemia and does not replace the five hour glucose tolerance test for Hypoglycemia.

YOUR DOC'S TEST FOR HYPOGLYCEMIA (OR LOW BLOOD SUGAR)

Five Hour Glucose Tolerance Test

You may want to have your doc run a five hour glucose tolerance test (plus a Hypoadrenalism, Hypothyroid and Hypopituitary test). Be darned sure it's a five hour glucose tolerance test, not a three hour Diabetes test.

A little tip: I've noticed five hour glucose tolerance tests are not always entirely accurate, 'specially if the person being tested is real skinny with a family history of folks that live a long time and have weird sensitivities. In that case, they could be a "Constitutional Hypo" who suffers off and on and may test out grade "A okay" one day and test out "Hypo" the very next day. I've seen these Constitutional Hypos do really well with the I.D.E.A.S. program of diet with supplements 'n' exercise.

Besides, every time I swallowed all that syrup for my five hour glucose tolerance test, I just passed out in about an hour—not much bang for the buck.

Five hour glucose tolerance tests are not always entirely accurate, 'specially if the person being tested is real skinny...

A SIMPLE AND CHEAP TEST FOR HYPOGLYCEMIA

The Livin' It Test

Like the self test for Adrea 'n' Al, a successful way I've seen folks self-test for Hypoglycemia is pretty simple and cheap. How do they do it? They follow the things outlined in this book, use the Relief Recorder for at least 30 days, and then keep in touch for support. Most get some relief in just a few days.

Many get some relief in just a few days.

CHECKIN' OUT CAPT'N TIM THYROID

Doing a Home Do-It-Yourself Test

How do I find out if Capt'n Tim is in good shape? Well Broda Barnes, M.D. outlined a simple do-it-yourself test in the Journal of the American Medical Association. In there she says folks with a laggin' Capt'n Tim stay cold a lot because they aren't burnin' up as much food as they oughta. So one way I check out 'ol Tim is check to see if my body temperature is lower than normal or I've got any of the symptoms listed back in Chapter 6.

Folks with a laggin' Capt'n Tim stay cold a lot...

All I use is a digital or basal thermometer (a regular fever thermometer won't do). I got mine at the drugstore.

Before I even get out of bed in the morning, I stick the thermometer in my armpit (not somebody else's) for 10 minutes. If the l'il' ol' needle says anything below 97.8°, the thyroid is low, all right.

Dr. Barnes has seen many people boost their thyroid by taking natural thyroid caps bought at a local health food store.

After someone decides to go the natural thyroid route, how do they know how much to take? Simple—they take one natural thyroid cap and poke the thermometer in their armpit the next day. If their temp is still below 97.8°, they take two caps the next day, one in the morning and one in the evening. In other words; they keep adding more thyroid caps, spreading them out all day, till their ol' bod gets up to 97.8°.

They keep checking their temperature till it stays at 97.8° for three days in a row. People using this natural method see many of their lazy Capt'n Timothy Thyroid symptoms go away. They keep checking at least once a week for three months to make sure their temperature is stable.

The ol' armpit test is described a lot more in Dr. Barnes' book, **Hypothyroidism, the Unsuspected Illness.** Dr. Barnes recommends natural thyroid, available at health food stores or through the Relief Network Mail Order Store—instead of prescription synthetic thyroid.

A little tidbit to remember: folks who check and find they have a low thyroid usually need thyroid, adrenal, and maybe pituitary support from then on. But, it's better than not bein' here at all, right? Besides, they say they feel so much better that nobody could get those Thyroid caps away from them with a gun.

Before I even get out of bed in the morning, I stick the thermometer in my armpit...

How Your Doc Can Check Out the Capt'n

For your doc to test Capt'n Timothy Thyroid, she/he may run the usual lab tests, T3 and T4 and TSH. (They sound like some model of a car or something, don't they?) Or, your doc may run the newer, more accurate test called 'FAMA', or fluorescence activators assay.[2]

ASK Doctor About Checking my thyroid?

Well, folks who've checked out Adrea 'n' Al and Capt'n Timothy Thyroid and have been on the I.D.E.A.S. for Relief program for a few weeks... and still feel punk, may check out the rest of their survival team. So they have their doc check out all these guys:

Harry Hypothalamus

Ovaries or Testes

Doc Pete Pancreas

Pat Pituitary

Arnold Thymus

Maestro Pineal

You may also want to run this test:

Candida-Antibody Assay

In Dr. Joan Larson's book, *Seven Weeks to Sobriety*, she reminds us to also test for all of these. Your doc will probably agree:

- chemistry profile
- amino-acid analysis
- hair analysis (mineral test)
- your blood count
- urinalysis
- food and chemical allergy assay
- serum histamine
- serum zinc & copper levels

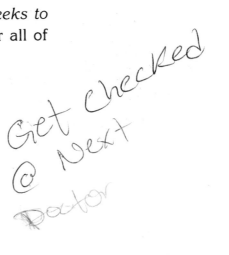

Just think—with one l'il blood sample, your doc can really help you on your road to relief.

REMEMBER FELLOW SEARCHER

All these tests are simply to help you find out where and when you need to make adjustments. So many times your engine doesn't need a major overhaul. A little tune up can get it running just fine.

You're really doin' great to come with me this far! Just keep it up. The answer you're lookin' for may be on the very next page, so keep goin'!

The answer you're lookin' for may be on the very next page, so keep goin'!

Chapter 8

A Word from the MDs

JOHN TINTERA, M.D. Dr. Tintera reports that many of his Hypoadrenal patients are perfectionists who drive themselves to exhaustion and then, because of blood sugar problems, some of them feel better right after eating, but not for long.

Some feel better right after eating, but not for long.

*...many were
misdiagnosed as...*

Schizophrenics

Manic Depressives

Psychotics

He goes on to say that many of his patients suffering from Hypoadrenalism have previously been misdiagnosed as Schizophrenics, Manic Depressives and Psychotics. He found most of them really perked up on an adrenal strengthening program, including adrenal supplements, diet changes, vitamins, exercise and meditation.

JONATHAN WRIGHT, M.D. Dr. Jonathan Wright, of Washington State, says he's found Hypoadrenalism among his highly allergic patients. "Since I became more aware of how to evaluate, test and treat folks properly for Hypoadrenalism," Wright observed, "I've had a lot less trouble with so-called 'brittle' allergic individuals. In fact, if someone comes in who has a whole lot of allergies, I'll almost automatically run the adrenal function test." (See Appendix A for tests)

"If someone comes in who has a whole lot of allergies, I'll automatically run the adrenal function test."

Dr. William McK Jefferies   Dr. McK Jefferies of Cleveland, Ohio, discovered that when he gave his patients' adrenal glands just a little boost, some of those patients made great recoveries from such ailments as Chronic Fatigue, anger, allergic disorders, respiratory infections, menstrual problems and even jet lag

Not only that, he said they showed no recognizable side effects from the adrenal boost. To quote Dr. McK Jefferies, "Because Hypoadrenalism causes Chronic Fatigue, sufferers are often misdiagnosed as having Psychosis or Depression. Tranquilizers, and antidepressant drugs, the usual treatment following this diagnosis, puts more stress on an over stressed body and can often make the condition worse."

Patients made great recoveries from such aliments as...

anger

Chronic Fatigue

respiratory infections

allergic disorders

menstrual problems

jet lag

These three distinguished doctors have shed a lot of light on Hypoadrenalism, which is often misdiagnosed. I have seen a lot of folks who think they have one thing or another who were helped by an adrenal boost, vitamins and exercise. The following story is a classic example.

I ran into a young woman in the grocery store recently who had been surviving on disability income for years under a diagnosis of Chronic Fatigue. Over the years I suggested she ask her physician for an adrenal function test, and each time she rather coldly informed me that "Chronic Fatigue is a brain disorder."

Thirty days after she tried the adrenal supplements, vitamins, and a sugar-free diet I had been talking about for years, she was able to withdraw from powerful prescription drugs and a new life opened up.

A little while ago, I saw her dancin' with her sweetie; she sure didn't look fatigued or whacked out on drugs.

A lot of folks who think they have one thing or another were helped by an adrenal boost, vitamins and exercise.

Chapter 9
Initiative

Initiative—n. A first move. (Webster's International Dictionary)

Now here's where the fun stuff starts—it really does...'cause in the next few short chapters you'll find out what you can do to get fast, fast relief for your pain, just like thousands of other folks have.

We're gonna start with Initiative—get it? Start with Initiative.

Initiative Test #1

If you passed test #1, great! Now you are ready for test #2. By the way, inhalin' and exhalin' is all that is required for staying alive—everything else is optional.

INITIATIVE TEST #2

Take a few minutes to fill in your Initiative quiz. Mark each item on a scale from one to five with a dot. Then connect your dots with a line, starting at A. and moving toward C. You'll see where the places are to add more Relief to your life. Giving yourself a score of three or more is great; giving yourself a score of zero is fine too!

A. I take action to keep myself in excellent health.

+ 5 4 3 2 1 0

I think, talk and read about health, and I never slow down in front of funeral homes.

B. I am at my desired weight.

+ 5 4 3 2 1 0

I'd be the right weight if I was two feet taller.

C. My blood pressure is normal.

+ 5 4 3 2 1 0

My blood pressure is normal for a 500 pound gorilla.

Now that you've finished the tests, take a minute to meet my mules.

We had a team of mules and three teams of horses around our cotton farm when I was a little boy. This was in west Texas...

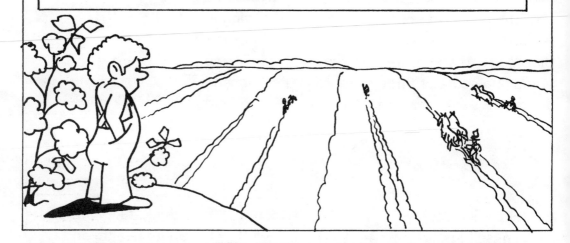

and the temperature could get up to 105° in the shade— AND THERE WAS NO SHADE.

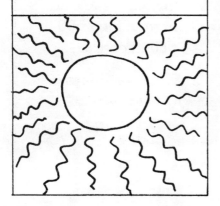

Those horses would keep right on plowin' until they dropped.

Not those ol' mules...

...when they got too hot, too tired, or too thirsty, they would just stop right in their tracks.

You could yank on 'em, beat on 'em, and curse 'em. They just stood there until they got some water and cooled off.

When they were rested, they would move on, just as calm as you please.

NOW THAT'S 100-PROOF INITIATIVE,
TAKIN' ACTION TO SAVE YOUR LIFE.

I figure a grown man like me ought to be at least as smart as those ol' mules, at least when it comes to my health.

Well, you took the time to read this far. Man, that's 100-proof Initiative.

> "...society encourages me to blame my emotional problems on people, places and things."

I look at how far I have come on my road to recovery. I'm tacklin' my emotional and physical problems as an 'inside job' when all around me, society encourages me to blame my emotional problems on people, places and things. Society says, "Blame, 'them' and take a pill. The pain won't go away, but you won't notice it."

JUST BEGINNING TO GIVE UP ALL THOSE OUTSIDE INFLUENCES AS THE REASON MY LIFE WASN'T WORKING WAS ONE OF THE HARDEST STEPS I EVER TOOK...

...so I had to take it piecemeal. At first, I was like a kid in a diaper, just learnin' to walk. You know, one step forward, two steps back, all the time clutching for anything to hold onto, anything to help me keep my balance as I explored a brave new world, searching for relief for my emotional pain.

In the early 1950's, there wasn't much known about lasting relief from tough emotional problems or alcoholism except "talk therapy." But like a baby, I had a goal. Every time one thing would fail, I'd get up again and try something else, grabbing anything I could find to hold onto to keep my balance.

Every time one thing would fail, I'd get up again and try something else...

I took the Initiative and I grabbed every book, every article I could find. I took the Initiative and went to every seminar that would help. I studied with every expert in the field of biopsychology I heard of. I kept the things that worked and tossed away those that didn't. I even studied megavitamin therapy with Bill W., the co-founder of Alcoholics Anonymous.

I kept the things that worked and tossed away those that didn't.

The days became weeks, then months, then years. I finally achieved a degree of emotional stability in my life.

Like that determined baby, I was so intent on reaching my goal I wasn't even aware of the changes that had already taken place for me to achieve a degree of emotional stability. In fact, for a long time, I wasn't really sure which changes had helped the most. Then it hit me—the only time I made progress was when I took the Initiative to try.

✱   I realized years ago that alcohol was affecting my behavior, but it wasn't until 1953, that I took the Initiative to stop drinking.

After I got sober, my behavior was somewhat better, but I was still subject to wild mood swings and terrible outbursts of anger. I soon realized that coffee affected my mood swings and I gave it up. However, I kept soft drinks and chocolate, both of 'em are high in caffeine and sugar.

"I soon realized that coffee affected my mood swings..."

"My addiction was so strong and my denial was so convincin'..."

It seemed my ex-wife would always know when I had been into sugar, colas, white flour or chocolate. "How'd you know?", I'd growl.

"Your fangs are coming down, and you've got 'that tone' again, and I'm scared," she would reply.

My addiction was so strong and my denial was so convincin' that it took three more years to quit the colas completely. It took more than ten years after that to give up the chocolate Häagen Dazs "cure" for depression.

I always told myself, "A little dab won't hurt," but I was totally brain dead about what else I had put into "the human disposal" (my mouth) in the previous days, or even previous hours, for that matter.

All this time, I was still smoking, completely unaware that all tobacco is sugar-cured and that every cigarette and cigar I smoked was loaded with sugar. No wonder smoking was so hard to give up, even when it was affecting my behavior—I was smokin' sugar sticks. Oh, I felt okay when I took that long drag (except for my cough), but I would panic when I couldn't find a smoke. And I would get really testy if I had to wait too long for another puff.

All tobacco is sugar-cured; every cigarette and cigar I smoked was loaded with sugar.

I tried for five years and couldn't stop smoking. But within 30 days after I found the right vitamin supplements and exercise, I just quit smoking and started exercising. That was over 30 years ago. As long as I take my vitamins, I seldom crave smoking, sugar, white flour or caffeine. And I haven't wanted a drink in more than 40 years.

It all began when I took the Initiative to decide what was right for me. Like those ol' mules, I just stopped right in my tracks and wouldn't let society push me another step in the wrong direction. That was 100-proof Initiative.

Initiative is an inside job that nobody can give you. Now, the question, "What can I offer you to make your first steps toward freedom less scary?"

30 days after I found the right vitamin supplements and exercise, I just quit smoking.

One thing I did was design a way for you to

keep a record of the changing you, called the Relief Recorder.

When you start keeping track of what goes into your bod, what your activities are and how you feel, you'll learn what affects you. Your bod is constantly changing; what doesn't affect you one time may zing you out another time. When you really notice what you're putting in your bod and how you're shaking it up, you can make connections between what you're doing and how you feel. Once you take the Initiative to really pay attention to how your body, mind and emotions work, you'll be on the inside track to a more joyful sobriety.

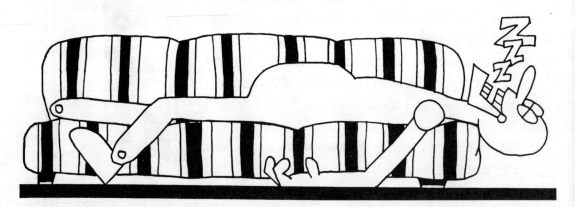

You'll really want to stay with your I.D.E.A.S. program, especially if you slip (oops) while keeping your Recorder. You'll have written in black and white how much worse you feel when you go back to those ol' couch potato habits.

Time	What You Put In	Activity	How You're Feelin'
Tues 8 AM	(A) Waffles, (B) sausage [H₂O glass]	Stretching Work at Computer	Good [faces]
	Alka-Seltzer ———————→		Tired! Sleepy Took Alka Seltzer [faces]
10 AM	———→ [H₂O glass]	AA Sponser Phone Call	[faces]
Noon	Stir-fry Chinese No MSG, No Sugar, Steamed No Oil, Rice No Tea [H₂O glass]	Met Chris for lunch	Good! They were glad to help [faces]
3 PM	Popcorn	Work Busy!	Hungry - Satisfied
	[H₂O glass]		[faces]
5:30 PM	Aerobics Class, workout		Sweaty & Satisfied!

Time	What You Put In	Activity	How You're Feelin'
6:45PM	Corn Pasta with Vegies, Caesar Salad, H₂O, Honey Ice-Cream (B)	Shower TV	Sacked-out
7:30PM	H₂O	Fight with Sam	Irritable, emotional Must be from honey ice-cream
8:00PM	Salt H₂O	Prayer Made amends 10th Step	
10:00PM	(C) H₂O	Meditation; Count my blessings! Made up all the way! Sleep	

In order for me to use my Recorder, I developed my own secret codes so I didn't have to write so much. Here they are:

A. Aminos I take first thing in the morning and mid-afternoon:
- 1 – 3 Lipotrepein
- 600 mg. Phenylalanine
- 1000 mg. Glutamin
- 100 mg. Tyrosine
- 500 mg. Acidophilus

B. Supplements I take with breakfast, lunch and dinner:
- 1 – 2 Adrenals   • 2 grm. Vit. C
- 1 B–complex   • 400 mg niacin
- 50 mg Zinc
- 3 multi-vitamins & minerals
- 100 mg. Pantothenic Acid
- 20 mg. GTF chromium
- 1 Evening oil of primrose

C. Bedtime:
- Calcium
- Melatonin

This symbol means water:

These guys mean:

your fangs are down

feeling low

tired

good

Great!

Six Quick Tips (not Q-Tips) for Keeping Your Recorder

1. Have daily/weekly/monthly/lifetime goals.

2. Be determined but not obsessed.

3. Work toward your goals one day at a time.

4. Be open-minded to new ideas and changes.

5. Be willing to take direction and take a chance.

6. Don't beat yourself up when you don't make your goal.

It's important to work with your physician, counselor, minister, athletic trainer, physical therapist,
your loved ones, and your higher power to heal
yourself.

Now, I want to take some time to help you learn
how to use your inner physician to heal yourself. So
take a minute to say hello to your inner physician, Doc Dumore, who's at work down inside you
right now.

*"Each Patient carries his own doctor inside him. We are
at our best when the doctor who resides within each
patient has the chance to go to work."*
—Albert Schweitzer, M.D.

Here's all there is to meetin' the Doc:
1. Hold your left hand out with thumb on top like you were getting read to shake hands.
2. Place the first finger of your right hand on top of your left wrist near the spot where your hot vein serves your left hand.
3. Feel that thump, thump, thump.

If you can't find your pulse in your wrist, don't panic! It's there or you wouldn't be here—so let's check it someplace else.
1. Place your first two fingers of your left hand on the right side of your throat under your jaw bone till you feel the thump, thump, thump...simple as that.

...feel the thump, thump, thump...

Doc Dumore has been beating this pulse for you ever since you oozed into this world and without any effort on your part.

Doc is always ready to work with your outside docs—and will give you undivided attention without an appointment. This book will help you put the right tools in Doc Dumore's hands so Doc can get the inside job done while you work with the docs who send you the bills.

Learning to give your own Doc Dumore the right tools and trusting Doc to take care of you is possibly life's greatest spiritual WOW!

And now...let's get into Diet.

Chapter 10

Diet

W e're all ignorant...only on different subjects.   —Will Rogers

Boy, was I ignorant about food's effect on my moods when I started my search for serenity 40 years ago.

I thought the four food groups were candy, cookies, pies and ice cream. My idea of a balanced meal was not droppin' my plate of fries at the hamburger joint.

So, when Doc Buxton started talking to me about changing my food intake to straighten out my serenity, I decided ol' Doc had flipped his lid. He just smiled and said, "If you can't unscrew

Simple sugars are in white bread, pasta, corn, catsup, soda crackers, as well as in booze.

your head and carry it under your arm, whatever you put in your body is going to affect the way you think and act."

Funny how we all accept the fact that alcohol, a "simple sugar" can make us act differently. In fact, we expect to act differently when we drink it.

Doc Buxton told me in 1953 that these same simple sugars were not only in desserts and colas. He said they were also in white bread, pasta, corn, catsup, and soda crackers as well as in booze. My answer was, "So what, Doc?"

He just handed me the only book on low blood sugar around at the time, *Low Blood Sugar and You* by Dr. Abrahamson, and suggested I follow the program outlined in the book and see how I felt.

Boy, I wish I could tell you I went right home, read the book and threw out all my sugar, but that's not the way it happened.

But, that night, over 42 years ago, I made a start and that's all I'm askin' you to do—make a start.

So, where do you start? Lets start with the food you put in. The one thing I've learned along the way is the food you put in can have two different effects.

Food can help you enjoy the view from the bridge or make you feel like jumpin' from the railing.

This chapter called Diet will help you to stay off that cold damp bridge railing and help you enjoy the view.

This little quiz is like the one in the Initiative chapter. After you mark each item on a scale from one to five and you connect the dots with a line, you will see where the opportunities are to add more sanity to your life and get that darned monkey off your back.

A. I eat regular, balanced meals.

+ 5 4 3 2 1 0

I select from the 4 food groups: cake, candy, pie, & ice cream.

B. My diet is low in salt, sugar, fats & caffeine.

+ 5 4 3 2 1 0

I'm a junk food junkie.

C. I eat some fiber (whole grain, raw fruits & vegetables) daily.

+ 5 4 3 2 1 0

Fiber—does this mean I have to eat cardboard?

D. I drink alcohol moderately or not at all.

+ 5 4 3 2 1 0

I never touch liquor; I just drink it straight out of the bottle.

E. I abstain from smoking.

+ 5 4 3 2 1 0

I don't smoke...but my cigarette does.

Supplements

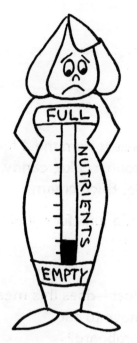

Anxiety and stressful situations of any kind often make you need more of certain vitamins and minerals, so you may have a nutrient deficiency.

Vitamins and aminos are called supplements 'cause we're supposed to get 'em from our food. Amino acids (aminos) are the building blocks of protein and essential to the human metabolism. I still take vitamins and aminos to supplement all the good foods I eat.

I found that starting a good vitamin/amino program helped me feel better so I was willing to learn how to eat for Relief.

Forty years ago my body was eatin' itself up on the inside because I didn't send down enough good nutrition. I had to start out on a detox vitamin amino program prescribed by Doc Buxton, and then move on up to about the second grade. After a few months, I was able to kick into a regular maintenance program, which I've adjusted from time to time over the last forty years. I've learned what works for me and my family and what doesn't.

I'm so darn glad you don't have to go through the trial and ERROR method like I did. It's not fun. Nowadays, there is an easier, softer way.

Right about now, you're probably saying, "OK, Bernardo—what do I do to get the 72 hour emotional relief you're talking about."

Well, the quickest and cheapest way I know of is to get off sugar and caffeine in all forms as soon as possible. Yes, that does include quittin' those good 'ol sugar loaded cigarettes (and all tobacco).

Robert Newport, M.D., is an orthomolecular psychiatrist (that means using vitamins along with talk therapy) in Santa Cruz, California. According to Dr. Newport, there are certain vitamins and aminos that'll help you stop alcohol, sugar, caffeine and smoking.

Dr. Newport says it's not only the vitamins and aminos you take, but how you take 'em that does the job. He also says that all alcoholics and usually their families have a certain vitamin/amino deficiency.

Anyway, I know of three ways to go about kickin' the sugar and caffeine habit for fast relief:

- The hardest—try stopping sugar, caffeine and smoking without vitamins/aminos for at least two weeks.

- Experiment with vitamins and aminos kind of like I did. Dr. Newport warns that occasionally certain vitamins/aminos can be toxic with some physical conditions, so he warns against experimenting without ongoing consultation with a knowledgeable medical professional.

- Try the easier, softer way and order one or more of the vitamin/amino relief formulas listed in the back of this book

After all these years I can still tell the difference when I forget to take my supplements, and those around me darn sure can tell, too.

WHEN YOU DO ORDER A RELIEF FORMULA

Let me tell you a little about the Relief Formulas:

- Dr. Newport endorses these formulas; formulas like these have been tested for years with thousands of alcoholics.

- You'll receive complete instructions on how to use your Relief Formula.

- You'll receive a caution list to check the vitamin/supplements you receive against your own physical conditions and medications you are taking.

- Best of all, when you open your box of supplements and read all the good stuff, if you decide it's not for you, just send back all unopened bottles for a full cash refund, no questions asked.

Remember, what I said, you don't have to buy <u>anything</u> to get some fast relief. Just quit sugar, smoking, caffeine and white flour. Also, get up and move your bod, man!

SAFE NATURAL "TRANQUILIZERS"

When my nerves are shot, I check out vitamins, minerals and other safe ways to keep my cool.

A case of "nerves" can often be triggered by nutrient deficiencies resulting from a poor diet. On top of that, anxiety and stressful situations of any kind often make me need more of certain vitamins and minerals, so I have a nutrient deficiency.

Some doctors say that many people who take tranquilizing drugs are on the wrong track. The right track, they say, can be as simple as changing eating habits. I know I'm much better off trying a safe alternative such as niacin, G.A.B.A. Plus or G.A.B.A. Calm. G.A.B.A. has no known side effects. Niacin does, so read on...

This concept of taking niacin is not new. Niacin, also called nicotinamide or B-3, has been used successfully as a tranquilizer for more than 40 years in certain psychiatric circles.

Niacin is a B-complex vitamin. We gotta have B-complex vitamins for our body, mind and emotions. These babies can't be stored in our bodies, so we've gotta get them from food and supplements. Get this little tidbit: B vitamins are *destroyed* by alcohol, refined sugars, white flour, nicotine and caffeine. Like I said, the B vits can't be stored in our bodies, so we depend entirely on our daily

Some doctors say that many people who take tranquilizing drugs are on the wrong track.

Niacin was an "orphan drug" because nobody could make much money on it.

diet and supplements to supply them. That's why taking niacin makes sense for many of us.

Niacin had the misfortune of being introduced at about the same time as the tranquilizer Valium, only minus the fanfare. "Niacin was an orphan drug, belonging to everyone because it was in the public domain," wrote Humphry Osmond, M.D., and Abraham Hoffer, M.D., Ph.D., noted authorities on orthomolecular psychiatry. "Consequently, it was in no one's interest to promote it by advertising or to advance it politically." (Journal of Orthomolecular Psychiatry, vol. 9, no. 3, 1980.)

Apparently, that is no longer the case. A research group from the Hoffman-La Roche company of Switzerland compares the vitamin's effectiveness to that of the minor tranquilizers.

According to H. L. Newbold, M.D., author of *Mega-Nutrients for Your Nerves* (Peter H. Wyden, 1975), "while most people feel better within days of beginning a niacin regimen, some require months to feel the benefits. It is especially important to give this vitamin a lengthy therapeutic trial because its potential benefits are so great."

Michael Lesser, M.D., author of Nutrition and Vitamin Therapy (Grove Press, 1980), agrees. "In using niacin, I begin with a modest dose of 50 mg three times a day and build up to the optimal level, the dose that achieves maximum improvement."

After taking niacin for a period of time—about two months—I got a blood test to check the function of my liver. Actually, this was not at all inconvenient since I wanted to check my cholesterol level too, 'cause niacin lowers cholesterol.

The tests showed my liver was doing a fine job metabolizing the niacin. For me and most folks, there is no problem at all. In fact, many docs, including those at Harvard, point out that a slight fluctuation in liver function tests simply shows that the niacin is doing its job. But for those folks whose livers have been damaged previously, the test might show that they should not take the niacin. The value of having this liver function test is another example of why I stress the importance of working with your physician.

Don't let my talking about the liver function test scare you. *First*, it's a very simple test. *Second*, most guys and gals show no problems. *Third*, especially when people use a niacin like the brand Endur-Acin[1], the low dosages are expected to pose no difficulties, as shown in the Harvard research. *Fourth*, folks like me who are generally healthy need to have the test done only one time to positively establish the body's ability to metabolize niacin properly.

After taking niacin for two months, get a liver function test.

Unfortunately, some folks shouldn't take niacin (B-3) at all.

Warning: Unfortunately, some folks shouldn't take niacin (B-3) at all. The folks that shouldn't take niacin include people with active peptic ulcers, severe liver disease, severe heart arrhythmias, diabetes, and gout. These folks should be closely monitored by their physician. Niacin is metabolized by the liver, and for some folks, that little bit of niacin might be the straw that breaks the camel's back. If somebody's been boozin' a lot for many years, his or her liver has been compromised and is not functioning as well as it should. If one has had a disease such as hepatitis or cirrhosis, the liver has been damaged and may not be able to handle the niacin, even at lower dosage. **Anyone with the above history should consult their doc before takin' niacin and should have a simple liver test every 60 days.**

CHANGING WHAT YOU EAT

After 30 days of taking supplements, eliminate the following *for at least two weeks*: sugar (see below), alcohol, chocolate, fat, fruit, fruit juices, caffeine, salt, white flour, and nicotine (every cigarette is loaded with 3 kinds of sugar), dairy and wheat products.

After two weeks, you may replace items, one at a time, keeping your Relief Recorder, so you can relate what you eat to how you act. Only then will *you* know which foods make *you* nuts.

I learned the hard way that takin' my vitamins, minerals, aminos, raw adrenal caps and gettin' exercise make it easier to leave the "legal drugs" alone.

Let's face it: you and I may be lifetime hypos (Hypoglycemic, Hypoadrenal and/or Hypothyroid)—but we're not emotional cripples. We can live free of those awful mood swings as long as we watch out for our old bugaboos. Here they are:

THE BIG FOUR PUBLIC ENEMIES:

1. SUGAR

2. CAFFEINE

- coffee
- colas
- chocolate

3. NICOTINE

4. THE FOUR PACK

- prescription drugs
- fats
- excess stress
- chemicals

Many of us think sugar is hidden everywhere—and we're darned near right.

PUBLIC ENEMY #1, SUGAR

Well, we're here at my old favorite, SUGAR— God, how I miss it. Did you know that sugar, white flour and alcohol are all considered simple sugars? They're just hollow carbohydrates that go directly into your bloodstream. They can cause memory blackouts and intense cravings. Boy, was I relieved when I found that out.

How did I become a sugar junkie, anyway? The truth is we alkie types break down all simple sugars including alcohol in our bodies twice as fast as other people do. You say, "so what?" Well, that puts a strain on ol' Pete Pancreas and we end up in a big ol' Hypoglycemic state.

That's the key to our addictivness. There is a biochemical error in our carbohydrate metabolism that is the underlying cause of our addictiveness.

Nobody has pegged which member of our survival team got lazy first, but the truth is anybody with this underlying metabolic screw-up is capable of becoming addicted to any substance that will give us temporary relief. This book is my best way of offering relief that lasts. I've tested it out for 40 years and it really works for me and hundreds of others who have tried it!

"Mental illness is a myth and emotional disturbance can be merely the first symptom of the obvious inability of the human system to handle the stress of sugar dependency."

—Drs. Abraham Hoffer, Allen Cott, A. Cherkaskin and Linus Pauling

Dr. Frederick Banting, who discovered insulin, tried to tell us back in 1929 that insulin was not a cure for diabetes, and that the way to cut down on diabetes was to cut down on dangerous sugar bingeing. It's notable that Diabetes dropped during both World War I and II when sugar was rationed and the number of cases of Diabetes has gone up ever since. It's simple. When you and I over-stimulate ol' Pete Pancreas with honey, fructose, refined sugars, fruits, and drugs (including marijuana), we become Hypoadrenal or Hypoglycemic, and LOOK OUT LUCY.

The way to cut down on diabetes is to cut down on dangerous sugar bingeing.

Refined sugar is EIGHT times as concentrated as refined flour. Hey, how about this: It takes 2½ pounds of sugar beets to make a mere 5 oz. of refined sugar.

Many of us think sugar is hidden everywhere—and we're darned near right. Almost everything that's frozen, canned or served from a steam table or vending machine has some form of sugar or a preservative that can make us hypos go nuts.

Then there's the sugar in booze. In whiskey, beer and wine the sugar content varies widely. When you combine all that sugar with alcohol, you've got a "real drain on the brain." It also seems that even sober alcoholics have an unusually high rate of auto accidents due to Hypoglycemia. So if you want to get there and back, to be with me, travel sugar free.

And don't get caught up in the health food mumbo jumbo—*brown* sugar is just *white* sugar wearing a *mask* made of molasses. Sugar is known

When we become Hypoadrenal or Hypoglycemic... LOOK OUT LUCY.

Brown sugar is just white sugar wearing a mask made of molasses.

Who'da thought bedroom troubles started in the dining room?

as sucrose, pure cane sugar, corn syrup, rice syrup, molasses, honey, fructose, Nutrasweet, Dexedrine, turbinado sugar, natural sugar, raw sugar, dextrose, liquid cane syrup, figs, dates, raisins, prunes, dried fruit of any kind.

So I read all those labels and ask the restaurant folks about sugar. "A little bit" of sugar is too much. It all adds up, doesn't have any nutrients and boy—will it affect my moods!

Well, how does sugar affect you and me, specifically? Us older guys and gals have a harder time with sugar, and when we mix sugar with tranquilizers and antihistamines, we're likely to nod off at the darndest times and not know what we've missed.

What about PMS? And I don't mean the Poor Me Syndrome. If you gals want to cut down on the PMS, cut down on the sugar. That's the way it's been at our house (and we're both glad of it).

For you guys, if ol' Mr. Happy stays sad a lot, cut down on the sugar and fat. Who'da thought bedroom troubles started in the dining room?

SUGAR AND ALLERGIES

As far as general food allergies are concerned, my teacher Dr. John Tintera tried to tell us way back in the '60s that the basic cause of all food allergies was our allergy to sugar. It's almost impossible to get anything made from wheat that doesn't have sugar in it (look at the chart where sugar is hidden right in this chapter.)

Another one of my teachers, Dr. Abraham Hoffer of Canada, said people with known allergies who suffer from depression usually got relief from their depression after he treated their allergies.

Then, there's dairy and wheat—most of us alkies are allergic to these two little jewels. In fact, according to some docs at Harvard, some alkies become allergic to anything booze is made out of, including corn, wheat, rice and potatoes.

And how about Kenneth Meyer, Ph.D., telling *Psychology Today* that "Aggression is an *allergic* response. This is a well-documented phenomenon that has been known to researchers since early in this century." I rest my case, y'all.

So now that I've made a case against the devil, what do you and I do to kick the habit? I started out by takin' vitamins and aminos like those listed in the Relief Network Mail Order Store. Then I cut that ol' devil out bit by bit. Pretty soon, I was lookin' back and waving good-bye to public enemy #1.

According to some docs at Harvard, some alkies become allergic to anything booze is made out of.

WHERE SUGAR IS HIDDEN[2]

Sugar Content in Teaspoons

12 oz. chocolate malt shake	18 tsp.
1 regular ice cream soda	12 tsp.
12 oz. sugar-containing cola drink	8 tsp.
8 oz. chocolate milk	8 tsp.
10 oz. lemonade	7 tsp.
12 oz. ginger ale	6 tsp.
8 oz. eggnog	6 tsp.
6 oz. cocoa	5 tsp.
1 piece apple pie	15 tsp.
1 chocolate cupcake with fudge icing	14 tsp.
1 chocolate eclair	10 tsp.
$1/2$ cup chocolate pudding	9 tsp.
1 small serving pudding	8 tsp.
1 small piece angel food cake	8 tsp.
1 cup vanilla ice cream	$7^{1}/2$ tsp.
1 serving sugar-containing fruit gelatin	$4^{1}/2$ tsp.
1 brownie	4 tsp.
1 small fig bar	3 tsp.
1 chocolate cookie with frosting	2 tsp.
12 oz. candy bar	9 tsp.
2 oz. penny candy	10 tsp.
2 oz. candied apricots	13 tsp.
2 oz. chocolate fudge	12 tsp.
2 oz. milk chocolate	8 tsp.
2 oz. jelly beans	$8^{1}/2$ tsp.
2 oz. lollipops	14 tsp.
1 baking powder biscuit, small	4 tsp.
1 hard roll	$4^{1}/2$ tsp.
1 slice white bread	3 tsp.
1 saltine cracker	$1/2$ tsp.
1 cup pasta, cooked	10 tsp.
1 average cinnamon roll	18 tsp.
1 cake doughnut, plain	$4^{1}/2$ tsp.
1 cup sugar coated cereal	8 tsp.
1 cup whole grain cereal flakes, sugar added	$5^{1}/2$ tsp.
1 white flour pancake, plain	$2^{1}/2$ tsp.
1 white flour waffle, plain	5 tsp.
1 tbs. pancake syrup	4 tsp.
1 tbs. jam	$3^{1}/2$ tsp.

PUBLIC ENEMY #2, CAFFEINE

Where is caffeine hiding? Did you know there is caffeine in soft drinks like Sunkist Orange, Mello Yello, Mountain Dew and in most root beer? It's also in diet pills and the herbal tea, Morning Thunder.

Let's look at some common stuff we put in our mouths and see how much caffeine is hidin' there.

Caffeine Content[3]

Brewed coffee	5-ounce cup	85-100 milligrams
Instant coffee	5-ounce cup	65 milligrams
Decaf coffee	5-ounce cup	3 milligrams
Tea	5-ounce cup	51 milligrams
Soda	12-ounce can	32 to 60 milligrams
Antihistamines	per dose	30- 60 milligrams
Anacin & pain killers	per tablet	32 milligrams
Midol	per capsule	32 milligrams
Excedrin	1 tablet	65 milligrams
Dexatrim	1 capsule	200 milligrams
No-Doz	1 tablet	100 milligrams
Stimulants	per dose	100-200 milligrams
Milk-chocolate bar	1 ounce	10 milligrams
Bittersweet chocolate	1 ounce	20 milligrams

"Caffeine is the world's most widely used mind-altering drug."
—Dr. Roland Griffiths,
Johns Hopkins
School of Medicine

"Caffeine is the world's most widely used mind-altering drug."   —Dr. Roland Griffiths.

That's what this doc said after completing a study on the addictive effects of caffeine. Caffeine is a non-prescription drug that's a central nervous system stimulant. Thirty minutes after putting caffeine in our mouth, it starts stimulating the central nervous system and constricting our blood vessels.

And talk about side effects! If you've ever popped NoDoz to stay awake or gone on a coffee binge, you know what happens—the jitters, can't sleep, nausea. Boy, do you know when you've had too much of the stuff!

What about good ol' decaf? Before you gulp, be aware that most production of decaffeinated coffee uses chemicals like methylene chloride also lovingly referred to as PAINT REMOVER (banned for use in cosmetics and hair spray).

Most decaffeinated coffee is made with chemicals like methylene chloride, also known as PAINT REMOVER!

Since we know that most hypos have chemical allergies which can set off depression or anxiety, why drink paint remover?

I know of a case where a woman in her thirties went to the *Ross Center for Anxiety and Related Disorders* in Washington D.C. because she was having panic attacks. She was having a bunch every day. The doctors did lots of tests (and oh, what a bill they sent her) and found nothing.

She was friendly, but fidgety, and talked a mile a minute. The center's director asked her about caffeine.

Turns out she was drinking two gallons of iced tea a day. The director encouraged her to wean herself off the tea—quick!

She called back a month later. She had gone a week without caffeine; the panic attacks were gone!

Caffeine is funny. It can make you wired or exhausted.

What's left that's *OK to do*? Try some of these caffeine substitutes.

- chlorine-free water (filtered, bottled, distilled or well water)
- unsweetened vegetable juices
- decaffeinated sugar-free colas
- Rice Dream
- soy milk
- say no to "sports" drinks sweetened with fructose

You may need to take it slow, but please, kick that caffeine right out of your life!

PUBLIC ENEMY #3, NICOTINE

Smoking Can Make You Crazy! No wonder I had such a hard time stoppin' smoking. Those darned cigars and cigarettes are cured with corn, beet and cane sugar—my God, I was smoking sugar sticks. A few puffs would get me up, then down, then I'd have to have more.

Well, 55 million of all folks in the U.S. of A. smoke. That's 22% of us!. Maybe it's the deadly insecticides in cigarettes we all crave so much, or the bleach in the cigarette paper. During the last 20 years it's estimated that 30 million folks have kicked the habit, including me. I didn't quit to stay here longer; I quit to make staying here more enjoyable for me and folks around me.

I do know that in my 41 years of working with

"If you're trying to quit smoking, watch it. Caffeine makes the symptoms of nicotine withdrawal worse."
—Harvard Heart Letter

alkies, at least one in every five of 'em who slipped had not been able to quit smoking, drinking coffee or dumping the sugar in. I'm also worried about so many alkies killing themselves *sober*—20%. Man, that's awful. And the Center for Disease Control says that high school students who smoke are 18 times as likely to commit suicide as non-smokers.

Chuck Tedesco at Smoking Release Associates has these tips for kicking the habit:

- Cut out the sugar, take nutritional supplements and boost your vitamin C & B complex intake.
- Drink at least 2 quarts of purified water a day.
- Pay attention to your breathing; breathe deeply.
- Try coping by massaging your jaw joints, between the eyebrows or the webbed area between the thumb and forefinger.
- Don't underestimate the power of exercise.

PUBLIC ENEMY # 4, THE FOUR PACK

Legal Mind-Altering Drugs

When I got sober in the '50s, a new "wonder drug," Librium, was the answer to all of our problems.

Then in the '70s, it was Valium, Xanax, and then Halcion. Now the "wonder drug" of the '90s is Prozac.

As late as January 1993, Consumer Reports reported that Xanax, Prozac and Halcion just were not effective. In fact, now they tell us that good old Xanax was not only more addictive than our old pal Valium, but Xanax actually causes rage and hostility. How about that, as if we didn't know.

All these drugs are recommended for bringing relief, but they don't allow you and me to get to the bottom of our problem. In fact, good ol' Prozac has replaced some "street drugs" as a way to get high—ain't that a kick?

If you are under the care of a physician, by all means follow his or her instructions. However, I learned that leaving off sugar and following the Relief Vitamin & Amino program I have outlined in this chapter turned my life around. At least these things I use are neither harmful nor habit-forming.

Deepak Chopra, M.D. warns us in his book, *Ageless Body, Timeless Mind* that "80% or more Americans are taking one or more prescription drugs today and four times as many are addicted to prescription drugs as street drugs."

Please don't make changes in replacing or withdrawing from any prescription drugs by yourself. Be sure you work with your physician.

Wonder Drugs of the...

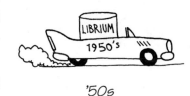

'50s

'70s

'90s

Fats

Hey you guys, I want to say a few words now about a word that catches more flack today then most any other word. I'm talkin' about the word "fat." Because fat takes more energy to digest, it can affect our moods and energy. However, fats are not our enemy.

In fact, we gotta have 'em for body fuel. It's just how we get 'em that counts.

If we just get our fats from what's in our food, not what we put on our food, we're usually okay, unless we eat processed food with fat in it. To get the latest dope on fats, read *Body Fueling*, by Robin Landis.

Stress

Stress is not a dirty word, but excess stress can blow a gasket. I raced cars for years. My race car was especially designed to handle a lot more stress than the car I drove to work. But every now and then, I'd put too much stress on my race car and POOF, out of the race just like that.

I'd put too much stress on my race car and POOF, out of the race.

We are designed to handle stress too, but like my race car, every so often we accumulate too much stress and POOF, we're out of the race.

You'll notice I said 'accumulate too much stress', 'cause we can still be carrying serious unresolved childhood emotional problems or emotional abuse by our mate or be all stressed out over money.

Every so often we accumulate too much stress and POOF, we're out of the race.

These little stressors don't just go away, they pile up inside and one day a broken shoe lace can cause us to call suicide prevention.

Now, changing diet will help us handle today's demons, but professional therapy, in addition to a sponsor, is important to kick those demons from the past out of our race car.

After all, with what you're learning here, you're going to be tourin' your race track at top speed.

If you're short of cash for therapy, swallow your pride and call the United Way or other organizations that will arrange a 'sliding scale' fee. I sent one guy to an organization like that, and he paid 50¢ per hour to visit a pro. Pretty cheap for checkin' out his wiring, right?

Chemicals

At the Health Recovery Center[4] for drug and alcohol rehabilitation, a study showed these startling facts about alcoholics they studied.

56% of their clients were overly sensitive to chemicals in the environment. So, you ask—what do I watch out for in the environment? Well, here goes:

- smog and air pollution
- scented things
- paint
- alcohol
- new plastics
- gas, natural and
  the kind used for fuel
- automobile exhaust
- new carpeting
- household cleaners
- chlorine
- cigarette smoke

Folks who reacted to chemicals suffered a variety of emotional reactions like fallin' asleep at the darndest times.

The Health Recovery Center further reported that folks who tested positive for any of these chemicals suffered a variety of emotional reactions like fatigue, depression, irritability, etc. or just fallin' asleep at the darndest times. Many of these symptoms look just like a so called "dry drunk".

So...if you have any of these symptoms...better check it out!

WHEN TO EAT FOR RELIEF

Ol' Doc Buxton kept saying to leave out the sugar of all kinds and eat basic complex carbohydrates like vegetables or grains, and/or protein every 2 hours.

I remember, this was 1953—I still thought the nuts in a Snickers Bar were enough protein and basic carbohydrates for a snack. The Doc might as well have been talkin' about me eatin' a shoe box.

I had eaten for years on a disorganized schedule called W.I.F.H., "Whenever I felt hungry." All this organization seemed like a lot to remember. My eating patterns used to go something like this:

The Old Bernardo Eatin' Schedule; Whenever I Felt Hungry (W.I.F.H.)

Monday

Breakfast	doughnuts
Lunch	bourbon and drugs
Mid-afternoon	Snickers, Mars Bar, or some other "nutritional gem"
Dinner	steak, potatoes and a few of those things called vegetables, "DADS" 32 oz. glass of iced tea and by God, my dessert
Late-night	that late night bulge builder, vanilla or chocolate

Tuesday   About like Monday

Wednesday   I don't remember, but it was just as nutty as Monday and Tuesday.

Forget the rest of the week 'cause I was just following the W.I.F.H. diet.

When Doc told me to eat vegetables and grains, he might as well have been talkin' about me eatin' a shoe box.

Doc Buxton got me started eatin' at regular times like this:

7:00 a.m.   amino supplements

8:00 a.m.   breakfast or protein supplement and vitamins

10:00 a.m. small mid-morning plus protein and amino supplements

12:30 p.m. lunch and vitamins with digestive tablets

3:00 p.m.   small mid-afternoon snack plus protein and amino supplements

6:00 p.m.   dinner and vitamins with digestive tablets

8:30 p.m.   protein supplement or snack

10:00 p.m. very small optional snack for "late-nighters" and, if needed, melatonin for sound sleep

"If you can't unscrew your head and carry it under your arm, whatever you put in your body is going to affect the way you think and act."

BERNARDO'S SUGAR-FREE FOOD PIE

Remember, one of the best parts of this, "Bernardo's Food Pie," is your occasional food splurges. So just go for it and if you splurge, don't beat yourself up 'cause that just creates Mars Bars inside...and here we go again.

Vegetables
Eat three times/day, 1 to 8 different vegetables.

Grains
Eat three times/day, two different grains.

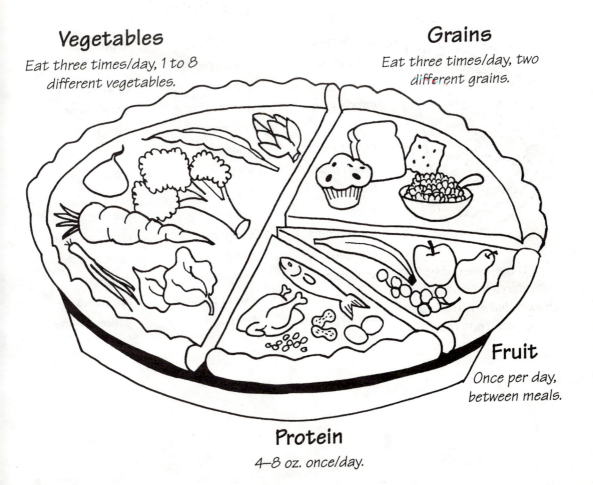

Fruit
Once per day, between meals.

Protein
4–8 oz. once/day.

Hey, the next pages are loaded with great foods to pick from[5]!

BASIC COMPLEX CARBOHYDRATES

Vegetables

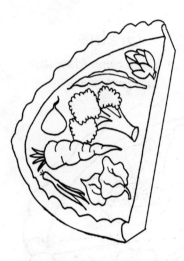

Eat three times/day, 1 to 8 different vegetables. Steam, bake, water sauté, or raw (not fried).

alfalfa sprouts	artichokes	asparagus
avocados	bean sprouts	beet
beet tops	broccoli	Brussels sprouts
cabbage	carrots	cauliflower
celery	collard greens	corn
cucumbers	eggplants	green beans
green peas	kale	leeks
lettuce	mushrooms	okra
olives	onions	parsnips
pea sprouts	peppers	potatoes, white
pumpkin	radishes	sauerkraut
scallions	snap beans	spinach
squash	sweet potatoes	tomatoes
turnip greens	turnips	yellow beans
zucchini		

BASIC COMPLEX CARBOHYDRATES, CONT'D.

Whole Grains, Beans And Legumes

barley
bran
corn
gluten flour
lentils
navy beans
pinto beans
rye
wheat

black beans
brown rice
dried split peas
grits
lima beans
oat
popcorn
sorghum
wheat germ

black-eyed peas
buckwheat
garbanzo beans
kidney beans
millet
peanuts
red beans
soybeans
white beans

whole grain breads, cereals, crackers, pasta. (No white flour or white rice.)

Eat three times/day, two different grains. Steam or bake.

Fruits

(dried fruits are too high in sugar for us)

apples
blackberries
fruit juices, fresh
guavas
nectarines
peaches
pineapples
raspberries

apricots
blueberries
grapefruit
mangoes
oranges
pears
pomegranates
strawberries

bananas
cherries
grapes
melons
papayas
persimmons
prunes
tangerines

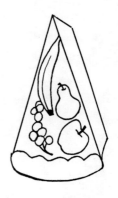

Once per day, between meals. Remember, for some folks, any fruit is too much.

PROTEIN SOURCES

beans and legumes   cheese of all sorts
poultry   plain or dairy-free yogurt
fish of all kinds

4–8 oz. once/day.
Steam, boil, bake, roast.

Many people want to limit red meat, since there is evidence linking some red meats to degenerative diseases and cancer—the high fat content is also a no-no. Red meats include: lamb, beef, pork, veal, and so forth.

Nuts And Seeds

(no added salt or additives)

almonds   Brazil nuts   cashews
filberts   poppy   pumpkin
sesame   sprouted seeds   sunflower
walnuts

Sorry, but sweets like pie, cake, candy and ice cream are really a fifth wheel on a four wheel car.

EATING FOR FAST RELIEF

You and I sometimes look for stress relief by eating. But many foods don't relax us, do they? Only carbohydrates (like veggies, grains and whole fruits) make our brain produce more serotonin, our calming chemical.

Foods to Calm You Down

• Eat carbohydrates alone. Proteins slow down the production of serotonin.

• Select low-fat carbohydrates like whole grain bread, rice and non-sweetened muffins. They digest easily and are a 30-minute quick fix to becoming calmer.

• If you can't eat, try a cup of herbal tea. It has more calming power than a couple of crackers.

• How many times did your mother tell you to eat more slowly? You will eat less and make the serotonin work better for you.

Foods to Perk Up Your Brain

On the other hand, protein foods like chicken, fish and dried beans cause your brain to make dopamine and norephinephrine. These chemicals make you alert. If you want to be really mentally sharp eat protein-rich foods. Lay off 'em at night for better sleep.

For That Lean, Mean Body Machine

Your lean choices are chicken, lentils, fish and shellfish, yogurt, veal, low-fat cottage cheese and dried peas and beans.

Be sure to have high-protein meals and snacks, but not too much, now! Three to four ounces of protein makes the brain produce dopamine and norephinephrine, the chemicals that keep you alert. Go ahead and eat more if you're hungry. But remember, too much food makes all your blood go from your brain to your stomach and makes you fat too!

Do you remember being told as a kid not to skip breakfast? Well, Mom was right. Eating a good breakfast is best. Your mood won't be affected, but your appetite will. Skipping breakfast makes you eat more at lunch time. Because you're hungry you load up on carbos and calories that make you go around in a funk.

You gettin' the idea? By the way, carbohydrates and proteins digest more easily when you eat 'em separately.

Do you remember being told as a kid not to skip breakfast? Well, Mom was right.

FOODS THAT CAN MAKE YOU FEEL LOUSY

- Dairy foods
- Wheat (and other gluten-containing grains like oats and rye).
- White bread
- Foods with sugar
- Fats.
- Alcoholic beverages.
- Coffee and other foods and beverages with caffeine.
- Soft drinks.
- Common allergy-causing foods like corn, peanuts and eggs.

REMEDIES

Sugar & Smog

If I get into sugar (or smog), I mix ½ teaspoon of baking soda in ½ glass of water and drink; or better yet, I take (2) Alka Seltzer Gold tablets in water. I Repeat in one hour if necessary—up to 8 tablets in 24 hours. This is not good to do every day, 'cause it's too much sodium for the bod.

IN CASE OF SUGAR (OR SMOG)

BREAK GLASS

ALKA SELTZER GOLD

Depression

I find 4-6 L-Phenylalanine (an amino acid) caps a day to be a quick fix for my temporary depression. Remember to check with your doc—this amino isn't good for everyone, 'specially folks with high blood pressure, cirrhosis of the liver or Schizophrenia.

Nobody's perfect, so the following are some quick fixes for sugar and food slips[6]. Check it out:

YOUR MOOD:	ARE YOU EATING A LOT OF:	NOT EATING ENOUGH OF:	A POSSIBLE QUICK FIX:
Depression, melancholy	Sugar, honey, maple syrup, milk and milk products, allergenic foods, over 70 percent grains (white flour)	Beans, fish, fowl, meat, whole grains	Something salty: umeboshi, olives, anchovies. Also aromatic spices or Alka Seltzer Gold or table salt
Fear	Sugar, honey, maple syrup, milk and milk products, allergenic foods; over 70 percent grains (white flour); meat, fats	Brown rice, barley, beans, cooked vegetables	Apple juice, kuzu (if tension), something salty like Alka Seltzer Gold or table salt.
Anger, short temper	Sugar, fats, salt, brown rice, cheese, meat, fried eggs	Salad, sprouts, sour food, kasha, corn-meal	A pinch of salt on your tongue, something salty, grains
Over excitement, excessive laughter, anxiety	Wheat, greens, raw food, stimulants such as coffee, chocolate, alcohol, strong spices, sugar	Seaweeds, kasha, salty foods, millet	Good ol' salt on the tongue, or Alka Seltzer Gold
Worry, lack of sympathy	Dairy products, sugar, sweets, honey, salads, sour foods	Sweet vegetables, millet, corn, cooked greens, fats, oils	Bread and butter

After you get the fire out, you can work on a long range plan (say two days at least).

Now that you learned a whole bunch of stuff about diet, see if you can spot the real myths:

Myth: *Don't eat too much bread because it's fattening.* Not true! It's the spreads that can make it fatty. But watch out for white bread: every slice is equal to about 3 teaspoons of sugar.

Myth: *If I eat more I'll get fat.* Not true if you stick to the six items listed below.

1. Start the day by eating sugar-free cereals or whole-grain bread and eggs.

2. Plan your meals with the vegetables as the main course instead of the protein. If you are serving chicken, brown rice and salad, add 1 or 2 cooked vegetables and serve less chicken.

3. Feed your munchies with carbos like carrot sticks, sweet bell peppers, cherry tomatoes and cucumbers. They're great crunchy foods to always have around. If you want to, use a non-fat dip or salsa to dress 'em up.

4. Use short cuts. Canned beans and chickpeas taste as good as homemade and take lots less time. Rinse them to get rid of any extra salt, and add to sauces, salads, chili, etc. Read all labels for sugar.

5. Remember the cruciferous veggies like cabbage, broccoli, cauliflower, kale and Brussels sprouts. They have loads of vitamins and minerals and are cancer fighters too.

6. Be creative! Look at your old recipes and see if you can find ways to add fruits and veggies to spruce 'em up. Don't overcook those veggies. They taste better a little crunchy and are better for you when you don't overcook 'em.

Myth: Potato and tortilla chips aren't so high in fat. False! Every 8 ounces of potato chips contain the equivalent of 12 teaspoons of butter—but boy they're good, aren't they? If you like to use butter, try the fat-free margarines available at your supermarket.

Myth: Fat-free desserts are a better choice than fat-filled ones. False! To help make up for taste, they are often loaded with sugar and have the same amount of calories as their fat-filled cousins. Because you are lulled by the fat-free label, you usually eat double or triple portions, which makes those damned mood swings even worse.

Myth: Sports drinks give you the carbohydrates you need for exercising. False! Don't buy that hype! You'd have to work out for an hour at your maximum effort or 2 hours at your normal pace to need that much of a quick carbo boost. The fructose in these drinks can be tough for your body to absorb, particularly during exercise, so you can get gas, or diarrhea and become bloated or even Hypoglycemic.

When I first started on this search for better health, I was so far down I would have had to get better just to be in good enough shape to die. I'll give ya a little tip: when we start messin' with our diet and taking vitamins, our bodies sometimes go through weird trips. Especially when stopping sugar, caffeine and nicotine. What we are doing is coming down off speed—just as if it were cocaine.

Coming off speedy things like sugar or caffeine or nicotine can make you sleepy, anxious, irritable, depressed, etc. I complained to my doc and he told me to take it easy, it would all come out okay in the end. He encouraged me not to quit when it got sticky and keep my diary daily so I could relate what I ate to how I was acting. I sure found out which foods made me nuts!.

It wasn't real easy, but after all, the only program that makes me *totally* pain-free is at my local funeral home, and I'm not ready for that.

Just look how far you've come. You've already learned about Initiative and Diet—so keep on readin' to learn how Exercise kept me and others out of that padded cell.

*The only program that makes me **totally** pain-free is at my local funeral home.*

Chapter 11

Exercise

The Unhealthy Health Nut

Back in the 1950s, my idea of exercise was to push my bar stool up to the bar all by myself, and my idea of living a balanced life was not to fall off that bar stool. As years went by, the more I sat on the stool, the more I had to sit on. If it hadn't been for the pickled eggs, fake cheese, and crackers on the bar, I would have "wasted away" to a heavy drunk instead of a fat slob.

When I crawled down from a bar stool for that last time in 1953, I thought that would be the end of my insane behavior, but boy was I wrong!

As the months and years of sober living went by, my wild mood swings and periods of depression, anger and violence were still there, although not as often. I tried everything I had learned about diet and vitamins, and I prayed and meditated. I spent so many hours with my shrink, he told me to stop coming. I got somewhat better, but something was still missing, and I had no idea what it was.

In spite of all the things I tried, I was still so moody that I couldn't predict how I was going to act when I woke up. I would get up at 5:30 a.m. go into the kitchen and gulp down some food so I could be civil by the time my wife and kids got up. Then, on Christmas morning in 1963, I accidentally discovered the power of exercise to affect my moods.

On that Christmas morning, for some unknown reason, I decided to take a little run with Liebchein, our 100-pound Doberman Pinscher. Now, most folks go through life livin' by the principal "Ready, Aim, Fire!" but I never could get that straight. With me, it's always been "Ready, Fire, Aim!" so, without a thought to the fact that I hadn't run since a high school track meet, I tied a 20-foot rope onto old Liebchein, put on an old pair of high-top Keds, and a pair of shorts that barely covered the lower 110 pounds of my 220-pound body. All this time, my muscle-bound running partner was leaping all over the kitchen, tugging at the rope.

The minute I flung open the kitchen door, I knew I had made a big mistake. I knew right then I would live to regret that I'd tied that rope on that dog— and would regret even more that I had tied the other end to my wrist!

Her paws sounded like a power lawnmower as she tried to get traction on the linoleum. Apparently, she felt there was a certain urgency to starting this run.

When she finally scratched her way to the kitchen door and leapt the four feet over to our driveway, I felt both my feet leave the kitchen floor at the same time. My arm grew six inches longer in a flash.

Across our front yard we ran, scattering snow as we dashed across one neighbor's yard and then another. Liebchein just kept diggin' in to get more traction. I thought, "God, she must have heard about the biggest bone yard on Earth somewhere down this street." I could just imagine some little blue-eyed tyke peeking out the window on Christmas morning, seeing this fat guy in his underwear sailing over their front yard, towed along by a giant animal. I could just hear his words, "Daddy, is that Santa Claus? Where is his sleigh, and where are his clothes?" After all, it was 1963, and nobody ran

across lawns in his underwear at 5:30 in the morning unless somebody was chasing him.

One of the habits I hadn't given up before I had this great idea to run was smoking cigars. By the time we crossed the third yard, my breath had not only stopped, it had gone back home for help. The trouble was ol' Liebchein didn't smoke. When I hollered, "Liebchein, NOT SO MUCH!" she must have thought I was callin', "MUSH!" and she just went faster. She seemed not only to have a destination, she apparently had an express schedule to keep—with no stops along the way.

By some miracle, Liebchein turned the corner, which finally brought us back home and through the wide-open kitchen door.

As I lay panting on the floor, my eyes bulged in my purple face. I could hear Liebchein yapping and jumping with joy.

As I grabbed the kitchen counter and pulled myself up, I felt something different—a new feeling of calmness, a sort of inner glow.

That morning, I was able to go in and have Christmas with my kids. They couldn't imagine why I could be so happy and crying at the same time. As I sat around joking at the breakfast table, I remember thinking, "It must have been the run that made the difference."

I ran the next day and it worked again, I was sane after I ran. But on that second day, I came to another conclusion: I had to either quit smoking right now, or teach that crazy Doberman to smoke. Well, she wouldn't smoke, so I quit. I had my last cigar Christmas day in 1963.

Most importantly, to stay sane, I have run every day for more than 30 years, and it still works every time. And what was once hard work is now endless pleasure.

After exercise I felt calm and able to have fun with my kids.

THE ADRENAL CONNECTION

I asked myself over and over: where did I get the energy to exercise that Christmas Day?

A few weeks later it hit me! Another one of my docs, Dr. Hill, was right after all! About a month before Christmas, Dr. James Hill, a nationally recognized endocrinologist, looked up from his desk and said, "Bernardo, you are going to notice an increase in your energy levels very soon with the vitamins and adrenal support I am giving you."

It was no coincidence that I was out there running in less than 30 days. Not only that, I had given up my precious cigars and cut back on sugar.

I learned *three* valuable lessons that Christmas Day so long ago:

1. For staying sane, any exercise is better than none—even if you have to lay down and roll.

2. Go from where ya are, with what ya got.

3. BE VERY PROUD AND BRAG A LOT.

Most of us are secretly scared of exercise: *"Will I look silly? Am I too fat or skinny? Will I keep at it? Which one should I do?"* Boy, I know how you feel—sooo, I have put together a simple system that will address your fears, answer your questions, and make you look goooood!

Moving Toward Exercise for Fast, Fast Relief

Step 1. Choosing the right exercise for you.

Step 2. Gettin' the right equipment.

Step 3. How to eat for it.

Step 4. How to warm up and cool down for it.

Step 5. Basic stretches for before and after.

Step 6. Measuring your heart rate.

Step 7. How to breathe for it.

Step 8. How to do your chosen exercise.

Step 9: HOW TO STAY WITH YOUR EXERCISE PROGRAM!

Start From Where You Are, but START!

The message is clear: you have to start from where you are, with what you got—even if that means a slow 10-minute walk or turning off the TV without the remote control. So let's see where you are and what you've got...right now!

Now's your chance to fill in your exercise quiz.

Mark each item on a scale from one to five with a dot. Then connect your dots with a line, starting at A. and moving toward C. You'll see where to add more exercise to your life. Giving yourself a score of three or more is great; giving yourself a score of zero is fine too!

A. I do aerobic exercise (run, jog, swim, dance, bike, brisk walk) at least 30 minutes at least 3 times a week.

+ 5 4 3 2 1 0

My idea of aerobic exercise is putting on my robe to get the morning paper.

B. I do stretching exercises 3 times a week.

+ 5 4 3 2 1 0

I stretch the truth about exercising.

C. I maintain bodily strength.

+ 5 4 3 2 1 0

My strength is a wonder...it's a wonder I'm here at all!

D. I am able to relax when I need to.

+ 5 4 3 2 1 0

My tension's all that's holding me together.

E. I get adequate sleep.

+ 5 4 3 2 1 0

I sleep like a baby: drowsy at dinner, wide awake at 2 a.m.

REMEMBER, FOR YOU AND ME, EXERCISE IS TO HELP US STAY SANE AND ENJOY THE TRIP. EVERYTHING ELSE IS A BONUS.

NOT ONLY SANE, BUT FIT TOO!

Scientists claim that bein' healthy and fit can slow the aging process. Aerobic exercise puts more oxygen into your body than any regular exercise, but ANY EXERCISE is better than NO EXERCISE! The results also show that people who begin exercising improve muscle tone, have lower blood pressure and *less depression*—all within the first six months of starting to exercise. It's never too late to start!

Exercises that force you to work against gravity like walking, jogging racquetball, tennis, hiking and aerobics help you preserve bone strength.

Strength-enhancing exercises like weight lifting increase bone mass and strength. This is really important because your bone tissue builds up to handle the stress of strength training. Not only do your bones, muscles and tendons get stronger but you increase your balance and agility. This lowers the chance that you'll fall and break somethin' you may need later[1].

Weight lifting builds the bones and increases your balance and agility.

Now, you've spent years gettin' yourself in the shape you're in today, so don't go expectin' to run right out the front door and tear off a ten-mile run on the first day. No sir! You gotta begin slowly. Maybe the first week you will begin by walking, the second and third weeks alternate walking briskly and jogging, and by the fourth week—all jogging. Whatever exercise you choose, take it slow. Don't expect to get your old high school pep back overnight. It may take weeks to repair your bod; in my case it took 75 weeks. You can, however, get emotional relief in just days or even hours. How about that?

The main thing is to stay with it! I guarantee that after a couple of weeks you're gonna look forward to exercisin'. Besides that, as your bod starts to feel better, your mind will tag right along. You'll be feelin' better about yourself and the folks around you.

STEP 1: CHOOSING THE RIGHT EXERCISE FOR YOU

What is Aerobic Exercise?

Aerobic exercise simply means getting your heart rate up to a certain level and keeping it there for a while. To qualify as aerobic exercise, your exercise must be nonstop steady for 12 minutes minimum. To gain the benefits of aerobic exercise, you gotta do it at least four times a week for 15–20 minutes.

Aerobic exercise is really important for cleaning your insides and getting out poisons or toxins through your skin. The skin is ol' Mom Nature's best cleaning agent, so the more you sweat, the better off you are. What a concept!

- **Aerobic Exercise** is defined as 12 minutes of sustained exercise at 80% of your maximum heart rate.

- To **improve** your aerobic fitness you need aerobic exercise at least 6 days a week.

- To **maintain** your fitness you need aerobic exercise at least 3 days a week.

- To **lose** aerobic fitness—cut your aerobic exercise to 2 days a week or less.

Your muscles do not grow while you're using 'em.
They only grow when they're resting.

Alternate Aerobic Exercises to Rest Your Muscles for Regeneration

Your muscle groups need rest between hard work, so you need to do different types of aerobic exercises and alternate them. The rule of thumb is:

If you are under age 50— Alternate the type of aerobic exercises you do in 2 day cycles. For example alternate jogging and biking or alternate swimming and weight training, etc.

If you are over Age 50—Alternate the type of aerobic exercises you do in 3 day cycles. For example alternate jogging, biking and swimming or alternate dancing, walking and weight training, etc. Without this rest you can actually lose muscle and bone, and we oldies can't afford that!

AEROBIC EXERCISE

Just look at all these exercise choices, but don't do 'em all at once! You may find it easiest to start off with walkin' or joggin', 'cause these are our natural forms of movement (unless you're a fish).

running

jogging

walking

x-country skiing

jumping rope

running in place

cycling outdoors

stationary bicycle

rowing

mini-trampoline

swimming

water aerobics

aerobic/step classes

roller skating/ blading

ballroom dancing

treadmill

NONAEROBIC EXERCISE

Stop and Go	Short Duration	Low Intensity

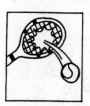

tennis

downhill
skiing

weight
lifting

golf

football

handball

yoga

TV without
a remote

raquetball

surfing

snacking

sex

dancing

STEP 2: GETTING THE RIGHT EQUIPMENT

The right equipment is important:

- If you choose water sports, the equipment for your eyes and nose are the most important (next to your swimsuit, of course).

- If you choose weight training, your back belt and gloves are most important.

- For just about everything else, your shoes are the most important.

- Break in your shoes gradually.

- Don't scrimp on aerobic shoes and don't wear aerobic shoes for everyday use.

- With a history of foot or leg problems see a qualified Podiatrist before you buy shoes.

- If orthotics (custom shoe inserts) are recommended, buy them and break them in gradually.

- For muscle soreness I apply Traumeel therapeutic ointment and place (3) Orinica 30x tabs under my tongue every two hours (I find these at my health food store).

Folks who get the good shoes first and keep a daily diary are more likely to stay with the program.

Now, tell me, are you having a little private conversation with yourself that goes like this?: *"I'll try walking and maybe a little jogging or aerobics for a while, but I'll see if I'm going to stick with it. If I do, then I'll get some good shoes."*

I've noticed that folks who get the good shoes first and keep a daily diary are more likely to stay with the program and keep themselves out of the "If Only" club.

Step 3: How to Eat for It

A suggested food program as well as info about vitamins and supplements is outlined in the diet chapter. However, most couch potatoes I've known got that way from lazy adrenal glands—if Andrea 'n' Al are lyin' down on the job, my potato buddies got them up off their shovels with a raw adrenal cap before starting goin' for it. The raw adrenals made exercising easier and more fun (They checked with their Doctor, first).

Extra special note: If Andrea 'n' Al or Capt'n Thyroid are weak, some people feel worse after exercising. They fix that with vitamin supplements and a Power Bar, but don't overdo it. They also drink plenty of water every 20 minutes during exercising, and a lot of water after they're done.

I've found that eating things like whole grain bread, vegetables and fruits give me the energy I need for my everyday exercising. Scientists have proven that these types of food give us much more lasting energy for exercising than foods high in fat and protein. Pretty simple, huh? Besides, carrots are a lot cheaper and quicker to fix than a hamburger.

Did your high school PE teacher talk about eating and exercising? If Teach told you to eat at

Be sure to drink plenty of water every 20 minutes during exercising.

least two hours before exercising and then wait for at least 30 minutes after you're finished, he/she was right.

To prevent a blood sugar drop after I exercise, I take a hot Epsom salt tub bath and soak for 20 minutes, then rinse off in a cold shower.

For more information see the diet chapter, and for even more information, get Covert Bailey's book, *Smart Exercise* (Houghton Mifflin).

STEP 4: HOW TO WARM UP AND COOL DOWN FOR IT

HOLD IT!
Before you start stretching you need to get those muscles warmed up—you could create pain. On a really cold day it's even good to have a hot shower (with shower cap) before you start your warm up. In order to avoid stiffness, it's a good idea to gradually cool down and slow down before stretching at the end of exercise.

Remember, while exercising 80% of the body heat you lose goes out through your head, so...

- To stay warm *before* exercise—cover your head.

- To stay cooler during exercise, uncover your head—protect with sun block and visor.

- Wear your sweats during warm-up; stretch before and after exercise.

- It can be painful to let your muscles get cold too fast after exercise, so stretch and cool down.

Some suggested warm-ups are:

- Walk briskly 5 to 8 minutes.

- Jog lightly for 5 to 8 minutes.

- If indoors—use a trampoline or bike for 6–8 minutes.

- Run in place for 8 minutes.

STEP 5: BASIC STRETCHES FOR BEFORE AND AFTER

It's a good idea to stretch for a minimum of 8 to 10 minutes before exercising and a minimum of 10 to 15 minutes minimum afterward.

Basic Rules:

1. Hold each position for about one minute.

2. Don't bounce.

3. If you have time for only one stretching session, stretching after exercising is best.

Calf Stretch

Start with your weight on your toes, heel up. Grip the floor with your toes.

Relax toes, let heel sink, regrip toes, relax toes and sink heel lower. Repeat till heel touches down.

Calf stretch in the open

Calf/foot correct position

DON'T!

Don't bounce that calf any time.

DON'T!

Don't turn your foot out or in — keep it straight ahead.

The Hamstrings

Start Here

*Here's where
the hamstring
stretch
starts.*

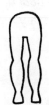

*The right
stretch*

DON'T!

*This is a wrong
stretch.
Keep hips level—
No bouncing.*

DON'T!

*Toe touching is a
no-no.*

Coming up from
hamstring stretch
Note bent knees
and bowed head.

Raise up,
knees bent
Straighten
neck and
back.

Legs straight
No locked
knees.

Additional
hamstring
stretch for
each leg.

Note straight back.

OPTIONAL

Quadriceps

A. Done on the floor or ground:

Side view of
stretch on ground

Front View

B. Done in the open or against a wall or tree:

*Standing "quad" stretch may be done leaning
against a wall or tree for balance.*

C. A third type of quad stretch—optional:

*Using a chair or table low enough to allow
for bent front leg.*

Additional Stretches for Running, Jogging and Walking

Thigh Stretch for Hamstrings

(Do both sides)

A MUST

Neck Stretch

Outer Thigh Stretch

Lumbar Stretch

(Do both sides)

(Do both sides)   *For Lower Back*

RECOMMENDED

Hip Stretch

Spinal Twist

For hip flexor

For Back & Sides
(Do both sides)

RECOMMENDED

Single Squat

Start here   Front view   Side view

To add strength to your front thigh and
loosen thigh after exercise.

DON'T!

Deep knee bend is
a no-no.

Don't confuse a squat with
the harmful deep knee bend!

Butterfly Stretch   Crossover Stretch

for Back and Sides
(do both sides)

Step 6: Measuring Your Heart Rate

What is your ideal heart rate during exercise? Use the chart below to figure out your pace.

Recommended Heart Rate During Exercise[2]

Age	Max. Heart Rate	85% of Max. (Athlete Training Rate)	80% of Max. (Recom-mended Training Rate	75% of Max. (Heart Disease History)
20	200	170	160	150
22	198	168	158	148
24	196	167	157	147
26	194	165	155	145
28	192	163	154	144
30	190	162	152	143
32	189	161	151	142
34	187	159	150	140
36	186	158	149	140
38	184	156	147	138
40	182	155	146	137
45	179	152	143	134
50	175	149	140	131
55	171	145	137	128
60	160	136	128	120
65+	150	128	120	113

Based on resting rates of 72 for males and 80 for females. Men over 40 and people with any heart problem should have a stress electrocardiogram before starting an exercise program.

The best place to take your heart rate is at any pressure point. The most easily used point is along the carotid arteries, located on either side of your throat. The pulse should be timed with a watch for a period of 6 seconds and multiplied by 10 to get the minute rate. For example, time the heart rate at the carotid artery at your throat for 6 seconds and count 12 beats. Then multiply that 12 beats by 10 to find your heart rate, which in this case would be 120.

Covert Bailey, the exercise guru, in his great book, *Smart Exercise,* has another simple way to figure out what "keepin' your heart rate up when exercisin" means for you. His idea is that everyone establish their pace—walking, running or jogging—regardless of the kind of exercise they plan to follow. You can find your pace by figuring out how many minutes it takes you to cover one mile comfortably and consistently.

We experienced runners define "comfortably" as moving at a pace that allows us to carry on a conversation haltingly. We should be breathing pretty darn deep, but not panting and gasping.

If you can repeat this exercise comfortably for seven days, Bailey suggests your "exact heart rate" isn't so important. Your heart rate is up, all right.

When you set your pace this way, you learn how you're supposed to feel while exercising. Knowing your pace keeps you from pushing yourself too hard, which is actually bad for you. How about that? I established my running "pace" more than 30 years ago and I'm comfortable with that pace for hours, even though I'm 30 years older.

Another accurate way of setting your pace is a series of treadmill tests, which is *real important* if you have medical complications.

STEP 7: HOW TO BREATHE FOR IT

Breathing is the key to exercise rhythm. When you see professional runners go by, watch their steady, flowing motion. Also notice how quietly they pass, how they seem so casual and how erect they are.

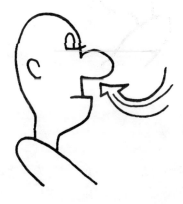

This all starts with coordinated breathing. For example, jogging is a four count breathing exercise. Here's how it works.

1. As your left foot strikes the ground inhale through your nose.

2. Hold that breath and put your right foot down.

3. Keep holding your breath and put the left foot down again.

4. Exhale that breath through your mouth when the right foot strikes again.

5. Start the process all over again.

Breathin' In

Always breathe in through your nose with your mouth shut. This will keep you from swallowin' any flies, and those little nose hairs are there to warm the air before it hits your lungs.

Breathin' Out

Breathe out through your mouth with lips puckered, and make a slight whistling sound.

- Joggin' is a four count exercise.
- Sprinting is a two count exercise.
- Aerobics is a four count.
- Water aerobics and swimming are two count.
- Rowing machine is four count.
- Weight training: exhale on contraction through nose, inhale on relaxation.
- Cycling varies, but on level ground it's a four count.

STEP 8: HOW TO DO YOUR CHOSEN EXERCISE

Lets start by looking at posture 'cause posture affects all parts of exercising. Correct posture helps avoid stress injuries.

First take a look in the mirror and see how you are standing right now:

Wrong way to stand

Right way to stand, walk or run

Now walk in front of a full-length mirror and see how you walk—most of us are unconscious of our stride.

Dangerous—do you walk with straight legs and your body parts out of alignment?

The best way is to walk or run flat footed, landing heel first, rocking up and staying forward on toes or all of foot with front knee bent.

Use an impact meter (sold in sporting goods stores) to alert you to problems with your stride.

Practice this way of walking several times, and try pulling with your arms while you walk.

Transfer your weight from your back foot to your front foot.

Now your back foot pushes your body forward, with your knee landing and your ankle extended.

Now your back foot swings forward to take your body weight .

Then there's pronation. This is how you roll your feet when you walk. The most potentially harmful rear foot motion is overpronation. Pronation is the natural rolling motion your foot makes with each step. Your heel strikes the ground at the outer edge and your foot rolls both forward and inward before pushing off with your toes.

If the inward rolling motion is extreme, this overpronation causes the bones of your knee to twist in opposite directions, exerting forces that can and usually do lead to knee pain.

Foot strikes   Foot flattens   Ankle rolls
surface on   inward on
outside edge   push-off

CORRECT PRONATION FOR
RUNNERS, BALL PLAYERS,
AEROBIC DANCERS, ETC.

Check your exercise shoe heels in the mirror.

BAD   GOOD   BAD

How to Check Your Pronation

You have three choices:

- Best—Ask a health professional, Podiatrist, or
  Physical Therapist to check you on a treadmill with video camera and design arch
  supports or orthotics, if necessary.

- Second Best—Ask a friend to check your pronation compared against the pronation illustrations to see if you have excessive pronation while you jog in place.

- Third Best—Look over your shoulder in a mirror to check your pronation against the pronation illustrations. (this can get tricky!)

Remember you should have pronation, not rubber legs.

Now that you know the correct way to warm-up, you are ready to choose some activities. Check out the information that follows to see which ones are right for you.

REMEMBER, IF YOU OVERDO EXERCISES, YOU CAN END UP WITH THE SAME SYMPTOMS AS TOO LITTLE EXERCISE.

YOU KNOW WHAT I MEAN—

HEART TROUBLE: DROP YOUR BUTT IN THE CHAIR AND NOT HAVE THE HEART TO PICK IT UP.

AEROBIC EXERCISES

RUNNING IN PLACE

Recommended by doctors for folks with high pulse rate, high blood pressure, leg or foot injuries, beginners, overweight and advanced age.

- You should begin this exercise under a trained supervisor to monitor your progress.

WALKING

A safe way to start exercising.

- Best for overweight and over 50 to start here.
- Best for people with history of heart problems.
- Best for people with leg or lower back problems.
- Great news for weight loss: jogging burns carbohydrates—walking burns fat.
- Aerobic benefit: 40 minutes walking = 20 minutes jogging.

If you don't get your heart rate up while walking, wear a back pack with enough added weight to reach your target aerobic pace and heart rate or race walk (for younger walkers) to reach your target heart and pulse rates

- When I have lower back pain, I check with a qualified Chiropractor and have him or her check my psoaz muscle.

Every 10 pounds of weight around your waist adds 50 pounds of pressure to your lower back—you may lessen that back pain by losin' weight.

RUNNING/JOGGING

20 minutes running/jogging = 30 minutes surfing or 40 minutes walking.

- Maximum aerobic benefit.
- Recommended time: 20 to 30 minutes non-stop.
- Pull with your arms—never swing your shoulders.
- Keep your knees soft.
- Heel first, push off with toes.
- Always run flat-footed to avoid injuries to calves, ankles, shins and heels.
- For permanent weight loss: run before eatin' in the morning.
- Drink plenty of water before and after (especially for folks over age 50).

AEROBICS/STEP CLASSES

20 minutes of step aerobic/step classes = 20 minutes of running/jogging.

- Only work out on a good floor.
- Work out with a qualified instructor.
- Keep your sweats on until you are really warm in class.

- If the music is too loud move over or ask them to turn it down—you can damage your ears.

- Dress warm afterwards.

- Prevent blood sugar drop.

SWIMMING

30 minutes non-stop = 20 minutes running or jogging.

- Great for heart and lungs.

- Be sure to protect against chlorine: wear water goggles, nose and ear plugs, and swim cap.

- I shower immediately after, then drink $1/2$ teaspoon baking soda dissolved in 4 oz. of water (or two Alka Seltzer Gold tabs dissolved in water) to neutralize chlorine.

WATER AEROBICS

30 minutes non-stop = 20 minutes jogging/running or 20 minutes regular aerobics/step classes.

- Appearances can be misleading—this is a real aerobic exercise and muscle builder.

- Do not experiment on your own—use a qualified instructor.

- Watch out for chlorine poisoning—always wear nose plugs and swim cap

- I shower immediately after, then drink $1/2$ teaspoon baking soda dissolved in 4 oz. of water. (or two Alka Seltzer Gold tabs dissolved in water) to neutralize chlorine.

- Take classes outdoors whenever possible for less chlorine exposure.

TREADMILL

Same as jogging or running outdoors, maybe better, less wear on knees.

- Most spas and gyms have treadmills that can monitor your pace, severity, time and provide you with hills or flat terrain. They even measure the calories you burn, your exercise heart rate and cool down rate. (It is even better to use a machine that makes you work both your arms and your legs.)

- Great for training: it's measured, controlled, and not as lonely as a country road.

- Be sure to wear running shoes and use all the warm-up and cool down pointers for running/jogging.

CYCLING

30 minutes bike = 20 minutes jogging

- Great for overweight or older people with back problems.

- Think safety: good helmet, lights, reflectors, traffic, ID.

- Indoor bike is just as good.

STATIONARY BICYCLE

A good way for older people and overweight people to start.

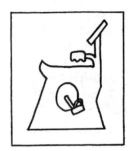

- Try one out at your local gym before you invest in one, as most of the "home ones" gather dust after a few weeks.

- You can get the same benefits as riding a bike outdoors with fewer traffic hazards.

- Downside is you're liable to stop too quickly and not maintain maximum heart rate.

ROWING MACHINE

30 minutes = 30 minutes running/jogging

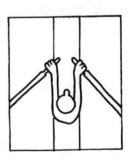

- This one always looks easy when someone else is doing it, but it produces some of the best aerobic benefits of any exercise—if you do it right

- Breathing, posture, and time are the keys.

- Ask a skilled trainer to help you sit up straight—no rounded back.

- Pull your arms all the way back each time.

- Put on enough weight to feel pressure.

- Remember your breathing: it's a four count.

- Recommended: 15 to 20 minutes non-stop.

- Start slow and build up.

- Always try this out at your spa before you buy one.

Mini Trampoline

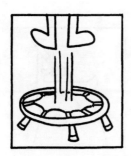

30 minutes = 20 minutes jogging

- Great indoor workout, particularly for beginners—gentle on the joints, particularly your knees.

- Wear good shoes, do not jump barefoot.

- If you have the instruction book—use it.

Ballroom Dancing

I'll bet you thought I put ballroom dancing on the aerobic list as a joke. Not so, my friend. If you really "get with it" regularly like my wife and I do, you'll get your heart beatin', I guarantee it!

So if your knees won't take jogging, your ego won't let you on the aerobics floor, and walking is too boring, too hot, or too cold, take a spin around the floor. Besides, it's the only aerobic exercise where it's OK to squeeze your aerobics partner. It's also a great way to meet other couples or maybe that someone special.

P.S. If you want to brush up, or look more like John Travolta or Ginger Rogers on the dance floor, look in your Yellow Pages and classified section for dancing instruction or dance clubs.

CROSS COUNTRY SKIING

Great aerobic exercise, equal to and maybe better than running/jogging since you use your arms more and tend to sustain aerobic activity longer.

- Just like running/jogging, the same warm-up, cool down, and stretching routines apply (see pages 166–172).

NONAEROBIC EXERCISES

BASIC YOGA FOR SHOULDER, NECK AND BACK RELEASE

Yoga is not a do-it-yourself exercise. You can't safely learn from a book 'cause you can hurt yourself either through ignorance or ego.

- Start out by taking a few yoga lessons from a qualified instructor.

- Don't rush it—yoga is not supposed to hurt.

- Yoga is not a competitive sport. Do your own level.

- Yoga is not about getting better. Yoga is about being present—now.

- Doing yoga in a class encourages you to do a full hour. At home we have a tendency to stop short.

- If you only have a few minutes each day at home, ask your instructor which four postures would be best for you.

- It is wise to warm up and do yoga stretches before doing anything complicated.

- Don't do yoga on a full stomach.

- Yoga actually builds strength. If you doubt it, try to keep up in a yoga class with some l'il ol' lady who's an advanced student.

I put yoga in here 'cause it's a form of meditation, and heaven knows we need to do all that we can to stay off the ceiling and out of the mental dumpster.

WEIGHT TRAINING

Weight training is not an aerobic exercise but it is an exercise that develops muscles, which are vital in aerobic exercise.

- Have a trained expert help you develop a complete weight training program that will tone your entire body and replace fat with muscle, without muscle or bone loss.

- Your weight training can be as simple as a sand bag, sit-ups, and push-ups, and chin-ups in your garage (be sure your knees are bent for push ups).

- Always wear a weight training belt (cloth, not leather, is best for support and comfort).

- Stretching exercises, warm-up and cool down are a must.

- Do not do weight training with injured muscles or back. If I get injured, I see a chiropractor and tell her or him that I'm lifting weights and follow her/his recommendations.

- To increase muscle mass use heavier weights, with fewer repetitions. To increase endurance use lighter weights with more reps.

- Women's muscles don't bulge from weight training, but their muscles *do* get stronger.

Remember:

- Pay close attention to your diet, vitamins, and adrenal support you learned in the Diet chapter.

- Exercise is not supposed to hurt, so take it easy!

- It's the time you *spend* not the time you *save* that keeps you healthy.

"Those who do not find time for exercise, sooner or later will have to find time for illness."
—Edward Stanley, Earl of Derby (1826–1893)

Step 9: How to Stay with Your Exercise Program

Starting an exercise program...that's a cinch. Sticking to it...well, that can get pretty tough for some of us. One key to maintaining your workout is to find a routine that fits easily into your schedule. Life, after all, is filled with piles of things to do every day. Figuring out how to cram exercise into a busy day may make you so exhausted, you don't want to do the exercisin' after all.

This l'il quiz can help you decide if the exercise you're thinkin' about using as your core workout (for example, walking, cycling, tennis) really works in your life.

Yes	No	
		My exercise can be done near work (or home).
		I don't need a lot of special clothing.
		I can do this exercise year-round or I have another exercise to substitute for it.
		I can do this exercise indoors.
		I can do this exercise outdoors.
		The equipment I need, if any, is minimal.
		The equipment I need is within my budget.
		I can fit this exercise into my daily schedule most of the time or will make it a priority item on my daily calendar.
		The exercise is not too time-consuming.
		I can do this exercise in any weather.

Mostly "yes" answers tells you that the workout just might work out. Look at the "no" answers and decide if these bad boys will keep you from really sticking with your exercise routine. If the "no" answers will keep you from exercisin', try another type of exercise, or maybe doin' it at another time. Above all, be realistic. Your choices about time, place, and the weather can guide you to a workout that works for you or help you find other good exercise choices.

Exercise with a buddy.

Try these ideas for overcoming "yes buts":

- *"I don't have time to exercise."* Combine your fitness program with some other activity: Read while on a stationary bike, walk on a treadmill and watch television, or shoot the breeze while walkin' with a friend.

- *"The place where I want to work out is too far away."* Find a workout routine that doesn't rely on out-of-the-way facilities. Work in the yard or garden. Walk in your neighborhood. Join a fitness center close to work. Buy a few exercise tapes and schedule an appointment with yourself every day at home. Or you can work out on some home exercise equipment[3].

Make an appointment with yourself to exercise.

KEYS TO KEEP YOUR EXERCISE PROGRAM GOIN'

- Get one or more exercise buddies.
- Join your local walking club.
- Join a local track or running club.
- Organize your own running club.
- Contact your local senior center.
- Join your local YMCA or your local spa.
- Join the President's Program for Fitness.
- Find an exercise you can do with your kids.
- Join an aerobics class (like Jazzercise).
- Get yourself some aerobics videos.
- Read fitness magazines for motivation.
- Try lessons for golf, tennis, bowling, or yoga.
- For more information, see Appendix C.

Throughout the years, I've learned a lot about exercise. First, I am convinced you and I were designed to move, or we'd be made of concrete. Second, it's simple arithmetic: if we don't burn off more calories than we take in, we're gonna to get fat. The third thing I learned from Paul Bragg, when he was still teaching aerobics at age 95: "If you don't use it, you'll lose it."

So start from where you are. Remember, you and I are exercisin' to stay out of the If Only Club. If we feel and look great physically—that's a bonus.

Chapter 12
Attitude

I'll never forget the time I was sitting in Doc Buxton's office bawling my eyes out, when I exclaimed, "Doc, I think I'm just a born loser!"

Big ol' red-faced Dr. Buxton looked across his desk and put on his most professional tone.

Think positive, Bernardo—think positive.

O.K., Doc, then I'm positive I'm a born loser!

Now that's what I thought a change in attitude was in 1953.

SO WHAT'S YOUR ATTITUDE SCORE?

Take a few minutes to fill in your Attitude quiz. Mark each item on a scale from one to five with a dot. Then connect your dots with a line, starting at A. and moving toward C. You'll probably get a pretty good idea of your current attitude... and no, you don't get extra points for scoring zero.

A. I am playful and laugh easily.

+ 5 4 3 2 1 0

I take my laughter seriously.

B. My concentration is good.

+ 5 4 3 2 1 0

My mind wanders and I don't know where it went.

C. I take responsibility for the quality of my life, including my fitness.

+ 5 4 3 2 1 0

Surely I can find someone else to blame.

You can apply all the diet and exercise you learned in the book and still be having a tough time if you aren't willing to change your attitude.

I discovered that I can create "candy bars" inside by the way I react to life. These internal thoughts trick my "survival team" into thinkin' I'm under attack, and trigger the emotional ups and downs. Although this books focuses on dealing with the physical side, I can only keep my joyful sobriety by dealing with my own attitude.

ATTITUDE OF GRATITUDE

The most important tool in this chapter may be an Attitude of Gratitude. The more grateful I am for what I've got, the less room there is for resentments about what I don't have. The more I appreciate this moment, the less I get into worry and regret. When I feel grateful, I'm more relaxed, my survival team isn't going crazy, and I can actually enjoy my life. See how feelin' grateful gets you goin' on a roll?

Acceptance[1]

Acceptance is the answer to all my problems today.

When I am disturbed, it is because I find some person, place, thing or situation—some fact of my life—is unacceptable to me and I can find no serenity until I accept that person, place, thing, or situation as being exactly the way it is supposed to be at this moment.

Nothing, absolutely nothing, happens in God's world by mistake.

Unless I accept life completely on life's terms, I cannot be happy. I need to concentrate not so much on what needs to be changed in the world as on what needs to be changed in me and in my attitudes.

—pg. 449
**The Big Book
Alcoholics Anonymous**

My friend Bernie Gunther used to say, "there is a positive and a negative side. At each moment you decide." I decide where I will place my attention, so I end up creating my experiences. I choose my own attitude, I am responsible for whether it is good or bad. Just as I choose to stay away from booze and drugs, I get to choose my thoughts. Choosin' healthy foods and exercise makes it easier to find those healthy thoughts, but I gotta decide to look for 'em.

Louise Hay has done some wonderful writing about accepting yourself...check it out on the next page.

Go to your mirror right now—not after you have lost weight, not after you give up depression or anger. You don't have to wait until you are living your Relief Program perfectly. Go to the mirror right now, look in the mirror, smile and say, "I love you"...
Smile, even if you don't mean it. I guarantee, your mirror will answer back, "I love you."

WAYS TO LOVE YOURSELF[1]

Do the best you can to:

1. Stop all criticism.

Criticism never changes a thing. Refuse to criticize yourself. Accept yourself exactly as you are. Everybody changes. When you criticize yourself, your changes are negative. When you approve of yourself, your changes are positive.

2. Don't scare yourself.

Don't scare yourself. Stop terrorizing yourself with your thoughts. It's a dreadful way to live. Find a mental image that gives you pleasure (mine is yellow roses), and immediately switch your scary thought to a pleasure thought.

3. Be gentle & kind & patient.

Be gentle with yourself. Be kind to yourself. Be patient with yourself as you learn the new ways of thinking. Treat yourself as you would someone you really loved.

4. Be kind to your mind.

Self hatred is only hating your own thoughts. Don't hate yourself for having the thoughts. Gently change your thoughts.

5. Praise yourself.

Criticism breaks down the inner spirit. Praise builds it up. Praise yourself as much as you can. Tell yourself how well you are doing with every little thing.

6. Support yourself.

Find ways to support yourself. Reach out to friends and allow them to help you. It is being strong to ask for help when you need it.

7. Be loving to your negatives.

Acknowledge that you created them to fulfill a need. Now you are finding new, positive ways to fulfill those needs. So lovingly release the old negative patterns.

8. Take care of your body.

Learn about nutrition. What kind of fuel does your body need to have optimum energy and vitality? Learn about exercise. What kind of exercise can you enjoy? Cherish and revere the temple you live in.

RELAXATION

That word 'relaxation' used to really sound wishy-washy to me. But now, I've learned to use relaxation. I even use relaxation instead of anesthesia when I have to have surgery.

We all want to relax in a hurry, so here's a type of relaxation you can do anywhere from your car seat to the toilet seat.

It's called breathin'! Breathe in with your mouth closed. Breathe way down below your navel then hold your breath while counting to seven.

Then, open your mouth, put your tongue against your upper front teeth, and breathe out slowly 'till you've counted to eight. This will make a whooshin' sound. When the air is all out, rest for one count, then breathe in again through your nose.

Do the complete breathing exercise at least 8 to 10 times. You're better off doin' this with your eyes closed (unless you're drivin', of course.)

Extra oxygen calms down the survival team, so your emotions get more calm too.

PRAYER AND MEDITATION

In my efforts to get sane, and have a healthy attitude, I studied meditation, and have practiced it on a daily basis ever since. I learned to get on my knees regularly. At first I was just going through the motions. Then I realized I didn't need to get on my knees to get God's attention; I already had that. I needed to get on my knees to get my attention. Gradually, my conscious contact with God became very real.

*I realized I didn't need to get on my knees to get God's attention; I needed to get **my** attention.*

TAKING A DAILY INVENTORY

Here's a little daily inventory form that I use. Feel free to make copies of this page and use it daily as an attitude check for excess, stress, or complacency. Remember, the quality of your emotional life is at stake.

Personality Characteristics of Self Will			Personality Characteristics of God's Will		
Yes	No		Yes	No	
		selfish and self-seeking			interest in others
		dishonesty			honesty
		frightened			courage
		inconsiderate			considerate
		pride			humility—seek God's will
		greedy			giving or sharing
		lustful			what we can do for others
		anger			calm
		envy			grateful
		sloth			take action
		gluttony			moderation
		impatient			patience
		intolerant			tolerance
		resentment			forgiveness
		hate			love—concern for others
		harmful acts			good deeds
		self-pity			thinking of others
		self-justification			humility—seek God's will
		self-importance			modesty
		self-condemnation			self-forgiveness
		suspicion			trust
		doubt			faith

HUMOR

Humor helps us keep our problems, big and small, down to bite size.

As you can tell, I really believe in humor. and it's no joke; research shows that forcing yourself to smile or laugh can help your emotions smooth out even when you still feel terrible inside. "People with emotional or physical pain often don't do things they would normally enjoy," says David Bresler, M.D., former director of the pain control unit at the University of California at Los Angeles. "They feel they can't enjoy themselves because of their pain or emotional disturbance. But it's often the other way around. Pain or emotional disturbance actually persists longer because they don't have any fun."[2]

The power of humor to heal is being tested at some nursing homes and hospitals. These places have "humor rooms" with funny videotapes, joke books, or cartoons.

Personal Relationships

You know, I've had cars that lasted longer than some of my relationships. My relationship with wife #3 involved two very self-centered people, and there was only one answer; she had to change. Well, I was willing to change as long as there was no discomfort, pain, hard work or embarrassment involved.

After I stopped eating the ice cream and candy bars, I noticed others around me seemed a lot easier to get along with. No big effort. I felt less jumpy and irritable. Of course, I wasn't jumping down their throats, or using a blaming/shaming tone...do you think that made a difference?

Relationships can be a big source of stress. And stress is another way to put our survival team into overdrive, taking us on that emotional roller coaster; then it's almost impossible to be reasonable and kind.

When we stress ourselves the survival team goes on overdrive; then it's almost impossible to be reasonable and kind.

The key thing I always remember is that I "stress myself". Nothin' anyone else says can make me feel anything. I can and do choose my reactions.

Relationships get stressful when I have expectations and demands. I only want them to do it my way, right? I can tell you from 70 years of experience that in relationships, I either "serve or suck". When I am making demands that someone else do it my way, I'm suckin' energy out of that person. I'm judgmental, controlling, and many other things on my list of character defects. When I'm like this, no wonder people want to get away from me.

When I serve someone, I bring energy to them. In real life, this means if I want the kitchen clean, I clean it; without complaining and demanding praise. Serving someone can be as simple as as bringing my sweetie a cup of tea in the morning. There's more on Service in the next chapter; it's the key to keeping *Relief* going.

Thirty years ago, I asked my sponsor why I went with so many crazy women. He said, "Who but a nut would want you when you're acting nutty?" As I worked on myself, I attracted more healthy people around me. I learned to get clear about what I wanted and ask for it with less manipulation.

I now give what I want to get: respect, kindness, affection. And I start by giving myself the acceptance I want from others; I'm a good person. My behavior may be unacceptable and need changing but I'm okay...and so are you, my friend.

Working on myself and my relationships also means keeping up the diet and exercise that refuel my own energy. You know, you can't give away apples if you ain't got any apples.

As I worked on myself, I attracted more healthy people around me.

Chapter 13
Service

This chapter is so important; I hope you can really take time to let it sink in. Service wasn't added as an afterthought to make the acronym I.D.E.A.S. come out right. Take five minutes to read the next few pages, then sit quietly for at least an hour and see what this could mean in your life.

SERVICE

Well, this is the last quiz and it's self-service. You already know the drill...take a few minutes to fill it out. Mark each item on a scale from one to five with a dot. Then connect your dots with a line, starting at A. and moving toward C.

A. I serve my family and friends.

+ 5 4 3 2 1 0 I barely have the energy
| | | | | | | | to stick up for #1.

B. I contribute to the well-being of my business, community and my society.

+ 5 4 3 2 1 0 I'm not with society—
| | | | | | | | I've been against it from the start.

C. I serve my fellow workers by being at my optimum energy level.

+ 5 4 3 2 1 0 There are days when I
| | | | | | | | feel like I just don't got nothin' for nobody.

Since you're my new old friend, I think I can let you in on a little secret: this whole book was created to provide me an opportunity for service to happen in my life—'cause I've learned that love and service are all that's real—everything else is just my darned SOAP OPERA.

Man, I know how it is to turn inward when I don't feel good—my medical history is ten pages long, single spaced. But that turning inward puts me right back there in my head again—right up there where the "If Only Club" meets.

Service can look like a lot of different things. I'm doin' service whether I'm smiling at a mom having a rough time with her kid or I'm reachin' out and 12-stepping a new friend. I know I'm doing service when I notice I'm not thinking of myself and I'm giving back to the folks around me.

We've got an expression in West Texas: "It ain't braggin if it's true." When you tell someone the truth about what it was like, what you did about it and what it's like now, you are carrying a powerful message, because this guy or gal may be about ready to crawl up on the cold, wet bridge railing and jump.

Service can look like a lot of different things. I'm doin' service when I'm reachin' out to a new friend and keepin' them off that cold bridge railing..

The ones who went back to the hurtin' had gotten fast relief and then quit doin' the things that made 'em feel good.

Service to others is something that came to me as a result of taking the Initiative to change my Diet and to Exercise regularly, which gave me a new Attitude. Then, wham-o, it happened. I wanted to share the miracle of my own life with friends, family and even perfect strangers just minding their own business. That's Service.

But get this: I've learned through the years that this sharing my own miracle with others has helped me probably the most. How about that!

Heck, I was a shy guy before I got the physical connection. I haven't found any way to get out of my head when I get into a stew except action. Lord, I've only got one mind. I can't think my way out of crappy thinking. I've got to act my way out.

I've learned my body, mind and emotions are all connected. When I reach out my hand to help somebody else, it pulls my head right out of my butt.

Over the years, I've seen literally thousands of good folks, from age 9 to 93, get fast, fast, relief with the I.D.E.A.S. for Relief. But my heart aches when I find out that many of those poor folks have gone back to hurtin' again. With each one, the story was similar.

The ones who went back to the hurtin' had gotten fast relief and then quit doin' the things that made 'em feel good.

The program is natural to your body and you don't get the high you get from drugs, so your mind plays tricks. Your Minnie Mind says "You're OK and so quit taking all that good stuff that's doing the trick." Those who really stick with the Relief Program

Reachin' out to help someone else pulls my head right out of my butt.

are the ones who share the miracle with others. In reaching out, these folks create a support group of folks who become partners for a new healthy way of living

It's easier to keep up the I.D.E.A.S. for Relief program when someone else is counting on you to show up for exercise or a nice healthy lunch. That's why I started the Relief Network. I also started it so others can carry on after I'm gone. The Network is a group of folks who have found a physical connection to emotional problems. We learn from each other, support each other, and gratefully do service for others. If you want to join us, share what you've learned with family and friends, then drop us a line; tell us how you're doin and how we can help!.

My message to you is: you can get fast relief by following what you've learned in this book. You can keep your relief forevermore as long as you share your miracle with others.

Thank you for traveling this far with me.

The Relief Network is a group of folks who have found a physical connection to emotional problems. We learn from each other, support each other, and gratefully do service for others.

Chapter 14

Conclusion

In 1953, when I first got sober, I was so antisocial my echo wouldn't even answer me back. The only difference between me and a "wet" drunk was I could remember where I parked my car. I was struggling to stay sober, to stay sane.

My ex-wife said, "You're not going to get any better. Why don't you go jump off the Golden Gate Bridge?" I said, "I'm going to get sane, dammit."

Shortly after that, my former wife passed on. She passed on down the street with a younger man. And I was more determined than ever to keep searching. And so it was, ten years later, on that Christmas morning.

The first big leap happened on that Christmas

morning in 1963. On that day so long ago, exercise became one of the keys to freedom from my emotional bondage. My gratitude for that freedom created a change in my attitude. That change in attitude compelled me to share my miracle with others, and that's how IDEAS was born.

Initiative: I took the initiative to quit drinking in 1953. and to gradually change my diet. I took the initiative to find the right doctors, and to take what I wanted and leave what I didn't.

Diet: Out of desperation, I had stopped alcohol, coffee, cigarettes, and slowed down on sugar dramatically. I slowly added healthy foods along with the right vitamins and adrenal support to correct any unbalances.

Exercise: On Christmas morning in 1963, after correcting my diet and using supplements for awhile, I added exercise. Exercise that started out as a "thing I did" became a part of me like an old friend.

Attitude: Because of exercising that Christmas day, my attitude toward myself and others began to change. I learned first to accept myself and then to love myself just the way I am.

Service: By golly, I found out that service is the key to permanent relief from emotional mood swings. I didn't realize it at first—it just sorta dawned on me.

KEYS TO A NEW LIFE FREE OF EMOTIONAL CHAOS

- Leaving things out: Saying no to the wrong food and drink

- Putting things in: Eating and drinking right for relief.

- Giving your mind a rest and releasing control: Daily prayer and meditation, relaxation and stress reduction.

- Learning "Cause and Effect": Keeping your Relief Diary regularly.

- Reaching out for help: Joining a support group or professional therapy.

- Playing it safe: Working with your physician or health care provider.

- Sharing your miracle: Providing service to others.

To My New Old friend:

So long for now.

Share the miracle.

Keep your Relief Diary.

Keep in touch.

Always,

—*Bernardo & the Gang*

Bernardo   *Claire*   *A.*

Chapter 4, How Your Survival Team Works
[1]*What You Should Know About Your Glands*, John Tintera, M.D.
[2]Renal means "of or near the kidneys."

Chapter 6, What Can Cause It
[1]*Journal of Clinical Endocrinology and Metabolism.*

Chapter 7, How to check It Out...Fast
[1]*What You Should Know About Your Glands,* John Tintera, M.D.
[2]available from Immune Diagnostic Labs, 10930 Bigge St, San Leandro, CA 94577
Tel: 510-635-4555.

Chapter 10, Diet
[1]Endur-acin from Endurance Products Co., P.O. Box 230489, Tirard, OR 97223.
[2]Calculated from tables by Bowes and Church, 1956.
[3]According to John Hughes, Psychiatrist, University of Vermont.
[4]*Seven Weeks to Sobriety*, Joan Mathews Larson & Keith W. Sehnert, M.D.1992, Fawcett
Columbine, 1992.
[5]*The Hidden Addiction and How to Get Free*, Janice Keller Phelps, M.D.
and Alan Nourse M.D. 1986.
[6]Adapted from *Food and Healing: How What You Eat Determines Your Health, Well
Being and the Quality of YOur Life*, Ann Marie Colbin. 1986.

Chapter 11, Exercise
[1]Adapted from *Your Health and Fitness*, April May 1994, American Heart Assn., Box
YHEW, 7272 Greenville Ave., Dallas TX 75231 & American Diabetes Assn., 1660 Duke
St., Alexandria, VA 22314.
[2]*Fit or Fat*, Covert Bailey. Houghton Mifflin, 1991.
[3]*Getting Fit Your Way*, Consumer Information Center, Dept. 108z, Pueblo, CO, 81009.

Chapter 12, Attitude
[1]Hay House 3029 Wilshire Blvd., # 206 Santa Monica, CA 90404, (213)828-6666.
[2]Adapted from "Jest for the Health of It", in *Your Health and Fitness*, June/July 1994,
Vol. 16 #3 p. 10.

Bibliography

Magazines, Journals

"Adrenal Suppression", *The Lancet*, December 19, 1987.

"Biochemical Factors in Impulsive and Violent Behavior", *The Journal of NIH Research, Vol.* 6, pp. 27-29, February, 1994.

"Do You Want a Cigarette, or Do You Need Nicotine?", *U.S.A. Today*, December 19, 1992.

"GABA, Nature's Remedy for Depression", Whitaker, Julian, *Health and Healing*. Vol. 3, No. 12, December 1993.

"Hormone Dependent Aggression in Rats", *Neuroscience and Behavioral Review*, Walsh, R.H., Albert D.J., 1992.

"News and Views on Psychiatry, Prozac, Suicide and Violence: An Analysis with Reports from the Prozac Survivors Support Group, Inc.", Breggin, Peter, *The Rights Tenet*, pp. 4-6, Winter/Spring 1992.

"New Scoop on Vitamins, The", Toufexis, Anastasia, *Time*, April 6, 1992.

"Orthomolecular Psychiatry", Pauling, Linus, *Science Magazine*, Vol. 160, April, 1968.

"Perils of Prozac, The", McLaughlin, Craig,*San Francisco Bay Guardian*, p.17, May 16, 1990."What You Should Know About Your Glands." Smith, Delos, editor, *Woman's Day*, February 1958. Reprinted 1993.

"Psychotherapy vs. Medication for Depression: Challenging the Conventional Wisdom", Antonuccio, David, *presented at the Annual Convention of the American Psychological Association*, Toronto, Canada, August 23, 1993.

Books

American Food Scandal, The. Robbins, William. New York: William Morrow & Co., 1974.

Body Fueling, Landis, Robyn. Warner Books, 1994.

Biopsychology, Pineal, John P.J. Allyson & Bacon, 1993

Bruised By Life? Turn Life's Wounds Into Gifts, O'Connel, Kathleen R., Ph.D. Deaconess Press, 1994.

Cooking for Healthy Healing, Rector-Page, Linda. California: Griffin, 1991.

Discovering the Physical Side of Mental Health, A Different Kind of Healing, Janiger, Oscar, M.D., and Philip Goldberg. New York: Putnam 1993.

Eating Right To Live Sober, Mueller, Ann and Katherine Ketcham. Seattle: Madrona Press, 1981.

Everything You Need to Know About Prozac, Jonas, Jeffrey M., and Ron Schaumburg. New York: Bantam, 1991.

Fit or Fat, Covert Bailey. Houghton Mifflin, 1991.

Guide to the New Medicines of the Mind, Extein, Irl L., M.D., Herridge, Peter L., M.D., Kristein, Larry, M.D. Pia Press, 1990.

Healthwise for Life, Mettler, Molly & Kemper, Donald W. Healthwise, Publications, 1992.

Healthwise Handbook, Kemper, Donald W. Healthwise Publications, 1991.

Healthy Healing, Rector-Page, Linda G., N.D., Ph.D. Griffin 1990.

Hidden Addiction and How to Get Free, The, Keller Phelps, Janice , M.D., and Allen E. Nourse, M.D. Boston: Little, Brown & Co., 1986.

How To Defeat Alcoholism, Beasley, Joseph. New York: Times Books, 1989.

Bibliography

Hypoadrenocorticism, Tintera, John W. Mt. Vernon, New York: Adrenal Metabolic Research Society of the Hypoglycemia Foundation Inc., 1969.

Hypoglycemia: The Disease Your Doctor Won't Treat, Ross, Harvey, and Jeraldine Saunders. New York: Pinnacle Books, 1989.

Low Blood Sugar and You, Fredericks, Carlton, Ph. D., and Herman Goodman, M.D. New York: Constellation International, 1974.

Prevention of Alcoholism Through Nutrition, The. Williams, Roger. New York: Bantam, 1981.

Second Communication to AA Physicians, A, Wilson, Bill. The 1968 reprint can be purchased from the Huxley Institute for Biosocial Research, 900 North Federal Highway, Boca Raton, FL 33432.

Seven Weeks to Sobriety, Larson, Joan Mathews, Ph.D. and Keith Sehnert, M.D., New York: Fawcett Columbine Books, 1992.

Smart Exercise, Bailey, Covert. Houghton-Mifflin & Co., 1994.

Somatics Handbook, The, Hanna, Thomas, Ph.D. Addison Wesley Publishing

Sport Exercise Injuries, Subotnick, Steven. North Atlantic Books, 1991.

Sugar Blues, Dufty, William. Pennsylvania: Chilton Books, 1976.

Sugar Isn't Always Sweet, Currier, Wilbur D., M.D. and Maura Zack. California: Uplift Books, 1983.

Sugar, Sex and Sanity, Yudkin, John. 1990.

Sweet and Dangerous, Yudkin, John. New York: Bantam Books, 1972.

Talking Back to Prozac, Breggin, Peter R., M.D, St. Martins Press, 1994.

You Can Heal Your Life, Hay, Louise. Santa Monica: Hay House, 1984.

Exercise Clubs and News

International Physical Fitness Centers Association
415 West Court Street
Flint, MI 48503
TEL: (810) 239-2166

Road Runners Club of America
1150 South Washington Street, Suite 250
Alexandria, VA 22314
TEL: (703) 836-0558 FAX: (703) 836-4430

Runner Triathlete News
3200 Wilcrest, Suite 170
Houston, TX 77042
TEL: (713) 781-7090 FAX: (713) 781-9594
area served: TX, LA, AR, NM & OK

Running Journal
123-B West Summer Street
Greeneville, TN 37743
TEL: (615) 638-4177 FAX: (615) 638-3328
area served: AL, AR, FL, GA, KY, LA, MS, NC, SC, TN, VA, WV, DC & MD

The Prevention Magazine Walking Club
33 East Minor Street
Emmaus, PA 18098

The Schedule (running & walking events)
80 Mitchell Blvd.
San Rafael, CA 94903
Tel: (415) 472-7223 Fax: 94150472-7233
area served: California

Appendix A

FOR YOUR HEALTH CARE PROVIDER

The tests for Hypoadrenalism referred to in this book were designed by three pioneers in the study of Hypoadrenalism: Dr. John Tintera, Dr. James McK Jeffries and Dr. Jonathan Wright.

They use different approaches to testing and treatment. Tintera does not think elaborate diagnostic tests are necessary to reach a diagnosis. "Diagnosis is possible by means of a careful endocrine history and physical examination rather than by laboratory tests."

Dr. McK Jeffries uses an ACTH test (the pituitary hormone that stimulates the release of cortisol) to confirm his initial diagnosis. In this test, McK Jeffries draws a sample for a serum cortisol test, administers 25 units of ACTH (he uses Cortrosyn because it is quickly absorbed) and measures serum cortisol levels again 30 minutes to an hour later. If cortisol levels do not double, the patient is considered hypoadrenal. Dr. Jefferies only moves into the treatment phase without testing when a patient is taking numerous other drugs. Depending on the sluggishness of adrenal response to ACTH stimulation, McK Jeffries will prescribe 2.5 mg., 5 mg., or 7.5 mg. of cortisol to be taken four times daily.

ACTH stimulation is an important part of the test because many hypoadrenal individuals, especially those in athletic training, can maintain normal serum cortisol levels in a rested state but have no adrenal reserve. After stimulation, cortisol levels in these patients sometimes don't rise at all or can sometimes even fall. The adrenal glands of these individuals are working just enough to keep up with normal activities, but they lack the reserve to respond to any additional stress.

Dr. Wright thinks the serum cortisol test does not give enough information. Instead of using a blood test, Dr. Wright uses urine samples 24 hours before and after ACTH stimulation to test a total of 11 steroids using a gas chromatograph procedure. This test allows Dr. Wright to see the levels and interactions of a broad array of steroids, making an informed diagnosis possible. According to Dr. Wright, "The serum cortisol test is useful as a sort of quick, hurry-up procedure. I found it a lot less useful than running a 24-hour urine. It is a lot easier to measure a broad range of adrenal steroids in the urine with the gas chromatogram."

Note: All three doctors agree that proper diet, exercise and meditation are important in the treatment of Hypoadrenalism.

Index

Relief Network

Mail Order Store   800-860-2579

The Relief Formulas

Most Relief Formulas will last a month. Each Formula has been tested over the past several years and is recommended by Dr. Robert Newport, M.D., Psychiatrist. The kits are proven effective for relieving the physical side of the emotional symptom indicated. An instruction sheet is included with each formula.

All our products have a money back guarantee!

Shipping—$4.50 on all orders

**Call and ask for special handling charges:
C.O.D., overnight express and orders outside the U.S.A.**

Relief Network News

This quarterly newsletter has the latest techniques for emotional relief, success stories from you, our network members and more! Featuring an "Ask Bernardo" column.

$12.00 per year.

ALL PRICES ARE SUBJECT TO CHANGE

800-860-2579

Relief Network Mail Order Store

	Item Description	Quantity	Cost	Total Cost
601	*Relief in Recovery*, **du Blanc** (book)		$17.95	
602	**Relief Network News** 1 yr (quarterly)		12.00	
603	*The Hidden Addiction*, Phelps (book)		11.00	
701	Basic Detox Formula		29.95	
702	Basic Health Vitamin Formula		29.95	
703	Basic Health Amino Formula		29.95	
704	Depression Relief Formula		29.95	
705	Anger Relief Formula		29.95	
706	Sugar Craving Relief Formula		39.95	
707	Fatigue Relief Formula		24.95	
708	Smoking Relief Formula		25.95	
709	Insomnia Relief Formula		19.95	
710	Stress/Anxiety Relief Formula		29.95	
711	Adrenal Booster Formula		19.95	
Subtotal				
Subtract Your 10% Network Member Discount				-
Subtotal				
CA residents add 8.5% sales tax				
Shipping				$4.50
Special Handling				
GRAND TOTAL	**Satisfaction Guaranteed**			

All Formulas are recommended by Dr. Robert Newport, M.D.

SHIP TO:

Name_____

Address_____

City_____

State_____

Phone (_____)_____

PAYMENT:

Check #_____$_____

VISA/MC#_____

Exp. Date_____

Signature_____

☐ It's OK to give my first name and phone number to MEMBERS in my area.

☐ Don't give out my name or number.

Make checks payable to: Relief Network Mail Order Store

Mail to: Relief Network, 1840 41st Ave., #102-177, Capitola, CA 95010

What is the Relief Network?

We are an international fellowship made up of women and men who have found a physical connection to our own emotional problems. We want to learn more, to hang on to our own joyful sobriety, and to share our miracle with others.

Discounts and Other Benefits

Members of the Relief Network get discounts on books and vitamins. Other benefits include sharing with kindred spirits. We'll periodically send you the first names and phone numbers of other network members in your area. We also hope to have a page on the world wide web!

You Don't Have to Buy Anything to Join

That's right! Just send us your name, address and phone number or use the order form on the previous page. Let us know if its OK to give your name and phone number to other members in your area. We'll never sell or give your name to any other organizations!

Sharing What We Learn

Start from where you are and share what you've learned with friends and family. Then find support buddies to plan regular exercise, have a healthy lunch or share literature about the physical side of recovery. Write us and tell us how it's going! If you write with questions, we'll do our best to get you answers.

Relief Network
1840 41st Ave, #102-177, Capitola, CA 95010